More Than Just Fairy Tales

New Approaches to the Stories of Hans Christian Andersen

Edited by Julie K. Allen

cognella®
academic publishing

For Niels Ingwersen, whose storytelling gifts rivaled Andersen's own and whose legacy lives on in the hearts of the people who listened to him

Bassim Hamadeh, CEO and Publisher
Michael Simpson, Vice President of Acquisitions
Jamie Giganti, Managing Editor
Jess Busch, Graphic Design Supervisor
John Remington, Acquisitions Editor
Brian Fahey, Licensing Associate
Sean Adams, Interior Designer

First published in the United States of America in 2014 by Cognella, Inc.

Cover image copyright© 2009 by Depositphotos / sabphoto
Interior image by Vilhelm Pedersen (1847) / Public Domain.

Printed in the United States of America

ISBN: 978-1-62661-018-7 (pbk)/ 978-1-62661-019-4 (br)

www.cognella.com   800-200-3908

Contents

List of Contributors

TOM LUNDSKÆR-NIELSEN

University College London

NATE KRAMER

Brigham Young University–Provo

SCOTT MELLOR

University of Wisconsin–Madison

JAKOB HOLM

University of Texas–Austin

KARIN SANDERS

University of California–Berkeley

JULIE K. ALLEN

University of Wisconsin–Madison

JAKOB STOUGAARD-NIELSEN

University College London

NETE SCHMIDT

University of Wisconsin–Madison

MARIANNE STECHER

University of Washington–Seattle

ELETTRA CARBONE

University College London

MELISSA LUCAS

University of Washington–Seattle

MAREN JOHNSON

University of Washington–Seattle

List of Works by Andersen

Listed in the order they are mentioned in this volume with common English translations of the Danish titles.

Mit livs eventyr (1855)	The Story of My Life
Fyrtøjet (1835)	The Tinder Box
Lille Claus og store Claus (1835)	Little Claus and Big Claus
Prindsessen på ærten (1835)	The Princess on the Pea
	The Princess and the Pea
Den lille Idas blomster (1835)	Little Ida's Flowers
At være eller ikke være (1857)	To Be or Not To Be
Vanddråben (1847)	The/A Drop of Water
Den store Søslange (1871)	The Great Sea Serpent
Om Aartusinder (1852)	In a Thousand Years' Time
	In a Thousand Years
	The Millennium
Hvad den gamle Johanne fortalte (1872)	What Old Johanne Told
Hvad man kan hitte paa (1869)	What People Do Think Up
Skyggen (1847)	The Shadow
De vilde svaner (1838)	The Wild Swans
Snedronningen (1845)	The Snow Queen
Historien om en Moder (1848)	The Story of a Mother
Taarnvægteren Ole (1859)	The Watchman of the Tower
	Ole the Tower-Keeper
Hjertesorg (1853)	Grief
	A Great Grief
	Heartache

Det gamle Huus (1847)	The Old House
Loppen og Professoren (1872)	The Professor and the Flea
	The Flea and the Professor
Kejserens nye Klæder (1837)	The Emperor's New Clothes
Den gamle Egetræs sidste Drøm (1857)	The Old Oak Tree's Last Dream
	The Last Dream of the Old Oak
Den flyvende Kuffert (1839)	The Flying Trunk
Pen og Blækhus (1859)	The Pen and the Inkwell
	Pen and Inkstand
Flipperne (1847)	The Collar
	The Shirt Collar
	The False Collar
Dryaden (1868)	The Wood Nymph
	The Dryad
Ib og lille Christine (1855)	Ib and Little Christina/Christine
Under Piletræet (1852)	Under the Willow Tree
Improvisatoren (1835)	The Improvisatore
Dödningen (1830)	The Dead Man
Svinedrengen (1842)	The Swineherd
Grantræet (1845)	The Fir Tree
	The Pine Tree
Den lille Havfrue (1837)	The Little Mermaid
Hyrdinen og skorsteensfeieren (1845)	The Shepherdess and the Chimney Sweep
Den gamle gadelygte (1847)	The Old Street Lamp
Gaaseurten (1838)	The Daisy
En Historie fra Klitterne (1860)	A Story from the Dunes
	A Story from the Sand Dunes
Hvad Vinden sagde om Valdemar Daae og hans Døtre (1859)	What the Wind Told About Valdemar Daae and His Daughters
	The Wind Tells of Valdemar Daae and His Daughters

Kun en Spillemand (1837)	Only a Fiddler
En Comedie i det Grønne (1840)	A Comedy in the Open Air
ABC-bogen (1858)	The A-B-C Book
Den grimme Ælling (1843)	The Ugly Duckling
Nattergalen (1844)	The Nightingale
Klokken (1845)	The Bell
Psychen (1861)	(The) Psyche
Metalsvinet (1862)	The Bronze Pig
	The Metal Pig
Tante Tandpine (1873)	Auntie/Aunty Toothache
Det Utroligste (1870)	The Most Incredible
	The Most Incredible Thing
	The Most Astonishing Thing
Paradisets Have (1839)	The Garden of Eden
	The Garden of Paradise
De røde Sko (1845)	The Red Shoes
Pigen som traadte paa Brødet (1859)	The Girl Who Stepped on Bread
	The Girl Who Trod on the Loaf
Barnet i Graven (1859)	The Dead Child
	The Child in the Grave
Paa den sidste Dag (1852)	On the Last Day
Engelen (1843)	The Angel
I Sverrig (1851)	In Sweden
Fodreisen fra Holmens Canal (1829)	A Journey on Foot
Gudfaders Billedbog (1868)	Godfather's Picture Book
Skyggebilleder (1842)	Shadow Pictures
En Digters Bazar (1842)	A Poet's Bazaar
Isjomfruen (1861)	The Ice Maiden
Jernbanen (1842)	The Railway
Den standhaftige Tinsoldat (1838)	The Steadfast Tin Soldier

List of Illustrations

Foreword

While most Danish writers, artists, and scientists of the early 19th century, the era of the so-called Danish Golden Age, came from the Copenhagen upper middle class or from idyllic parsonages on the island of Zealand, Hans Christian Andersen (1805-75)—who knew and befriended most of the former—came from the dregs of society. His mother was an alcoholic washerwoman and his father an impoverished shoemaker. They lived in the provincial town of Odense on the island of Funen. Although Andersen himself never disguised his background, despite moving in bourgeois and aristocratic circles all over Europe for much of his adult life, he nevertheless grappled with a number of social challenges that contributed to both the many tensions and discordant elements to be found in his works as well as his numerous unsuccessful love affairs. These traumas left a definite trace in his writings, which is one of the reasons Andersen's oeuvre—including his tales and stories—goes far beyond traditional children's literature. By exploring how these social issues manifest themselves in Andersen's tales, the present volume challenges the widespread misconception that Andersen's works are primarily, let alone exclusively, for children and offers readers an array of models for recognizing the connections between many of Andersen's tales and interpreting the deeper significance and contextual significance of these patterns.

Andersen's own life story resembles a fairy tale in many ways, at least in terms of his unexpected rise to fame and fortune; indeed, he titled his first autobiography *Mit Livs Eventyr* (*The Fairy Tale of My Life*, 1855). In an 1833 letter, Andersen described himself as a "swamp plant,"[1] an accurate description of the poverty, alcoholism, and promiscuity that characterized his family background and social environment in childhood. However, the factual information Andersen gives about his parents and their background in his various autobiographies is very limited, and totally unfounded theories have been proposed, claiming that Andersen was either the child of a French immigrant or the illegitimate son of Prince Christian Frederik, later King Christian VIII. Even though the limited schooling he received in Odense did not teach him how to spell and write without errors, Andersen devoured any book he could get hold of, from the Danish classics to William Shakespeare, and learned whole passages and scenes by heart. In 1812, when Andersen was only seven, his parents took him to the local

---

1   In a letter to Henriette Wulff on February 16, 1833. *Breve fra Hans Christian Andersen*, vol. 1, edited by C. St. A. Bille and Nicolai Bøgh. Copenhagen: Gyldendal, 1878, p. 114.

theater for the first time to see comic operas or singspiels and he already began dreaming of a theatrical career.

Andersen always had a strong sense of his own destiny, despite the obstacles in his path. Following his confirmation in the Lutheran church in 1819, various local prominent people who had taken an interest in the talented boy urged Andersen's mother to let him learn a trade. She wanted him apprenticed to a tailor, but he would have none of it. His fondness for the theater had steadily increased during these years—in 1818 when the Royal Theater visited Odense, he was given a walk-on part and a few lines to speak—and he was determined to become an actor in Copenhagen. In the end Andersen's mother gave in, but only after she had consulted a fortune-teller, who predicted that her son would become a great man and that Odense would one day be lit up in his honor. In response to his worried mother's exclamation, "Whatever will become of you there?" Andersen—according to his autobiography—confidently replied, "I shall become famous!"[2] On September 4, 1819, Andersen left Odense and two days later, after having traveled as a stowaway, arrived in the Danish capital.

Contrary to his own expectations, Andersen did not succeed in conquering the Danish stage either as an actor or as a playwright and was advised to return home. With characteristic stubbornness and against all odds, he embarked instead on a career as a poet, influenced by the *Weltschmerz* (world-weariness) and discordance found in the works of the immensely popular German writer Heinrich Heine. Andersen's poems turned him into a great local success. Throughout his life he continued to publish poetry—partly poems of ideas and partly poems written for various public and private occasions—and a similar *Zerissenheit* (fragmentation) can be found in a number of underrated novels and dramas he wrote in the 1830s and 1840s, works that in Andersen's own time made him famous but today unfortunately are familiar primarily to a small Danish audience.

It was not until after having returned from Italy on his first major journey abroad in 1833-34—all together Andersen traveled abroad thirty times and was thus one of the greatest travelers of his time—that he achieved his artistic as well as international commercial breakthrough. In Italy he had collected material for his partly autobiographical novel *Improvisatoren* (*The Improvisatore*, 1835). Simultaneously, he had started a new project, as he casually informed a friend in a letter written New Year's Day, 1835: "Now I shall begin to write some 'fairy tales for children.' I want to win the coming generations, you see."[3] On May 8, 1835, a slim volume, *Eventyr, fortalte for Børn* (*Tales, Told for Children*) containing "Fyrtøiet" ("The Tinderbox"), "Lille Claus og store Claus" ("Little Claus and Big Claus"), "Prindsessen paa Ærten" ("The Princess on the Pea"), and "Den lille Idas Blomster" ("Little Ida's Flowers") was published. In the opinion of the critics, these tales were completely unsuitable for

---

2 *Mit Livs Eventyr*, 1, p. 27. All quotes from *Mit Livs Eventyr*, 1–2, are from *Samlede Skrifter*, 1, 2d ed. Copenhagen: C. A. Reitzel, 1876.

3 *H. C. Andersens Brevveksling med Henriette Hanck*. 1830–1846. In: *Anderseniana*, 10, edited by Svend Larsen. Copenhagen: Munksgaard, 1941–46,, p. 104.

children, because they were immoral and without pedagogical value. In addition, the style was condemned as being too colloquial.

The first three of the 156 tales and stories Andersen wrote were rather straightforwardly rewritten folk tales. Gradually, however, he developed his own unique universe with immensely artistic and philosophical complexity that to this day continues to challenge and fascinate scholars, as the present volume exemplifies. The first six collections of Andersen's fairy tales, from 1835 to 1841, were subtitled "Told for Children," which reveals Andersen's ingenious discovery that his tales had to be *told*. The tales themselves seem so simple, but the original manuscripts confirm Andersen's patient, meticulous efforts to find—or create, if necessary—the exact expressions that fit his intention in each tale. As a mature author, Andersen began to write texts of greater length and of a different, more realistic nature and thus the two collections of 1852–53 bear the title *Historier* (*Stories*). Andersen did not give up the fairy tale genre, however, and his last eleven volumes, from 1858 to 1872, are entitled *Eventyr og Historier* (*Fairy Tales and Stories*).

It is important to keep in mind that Andersen lived and wrote during two contrasting literary periods of the 19th century: romanticism and realism/naturalism. The clash between these two schools of philosophical thought and literary style constitute next to the social and linguistic components yet another significant and fascinating feature of his writing and is to a certain degree reflected in the two genres used by Andersen: the fairy tale and the short story. He was well aware of his position between two ideologies. Thus he was familiar with the radical theology of David Friedrich Strauss and Ludwig Feuerbach; he discusses and rejects the theories contained in Karl Marx' *Das kommunistische Manifest* (*The Communist Manifesto*, 1848) in his late novel *At være eller ikke være* (*To Be or Not to Be*, 1857), as posing an imminent danger to the romantic idealism he could not do without.

Nevertheless, Andersen was an admirer of modern technology—in the tale "Vanddraaben" ("A Drop of Water," 1848) he describes a microscope; in "Den store Søeslange" ("The Great Sea-Serpent," 1872) he writes about the telegraph cable under the Atlantic Ocean; he even ventures as far as fantasizing, in the science fiction story "Om Aartusinder" ("In a Thousand Years' Time," 1852), about a group of busy young Americans flying to Europe on the wings of steam with only eight days to spend, a remarkable anticipation of Jules Verne's novel, *Le Tour du monde en quatre-vingt jours* ("A Trip Around the World in Eighty Days," 1873). However, in instances where Andersen felt that progress would entail a victory of matter over spirit, he would adamantly hit the brakes. In such cases he would admonish his audience, as expressed in the story "Hvad den gamle Johanne fortalte" ("What Old Johanne Told," 1872): "Say the Lord's Prayer!"

At the same time, Andersen—the first proletarian of Danish literature—was well aware that the good *old* days were not necessarily the *good* old days. This is how the old woman in the tale—or perhaps rather short story—"Hvad man kan hitte paa" ("What People Do Think Up," 1869) reacts to the longing for the past of a young man who wishes to become a writer: "In the old days, wise old women were burned alive, and poets went around with hollow bellies and their elbows sticking out of their sleeves. The times are in fact good; they are the best of all times! But you don't have the right way of looking at them. You don't use your ears, and"—and now we see Andersen's admonishing index finger wagging at us—"you're probably not saying the Lord's Prayer at night."[4] Thus, it is all right for a writer to practice realism, but the metaphysical aspect must *not* be ignored.

It is precisely in the contrast between idealism und realism that we find yet another fundamental tension, a philosophical dualism, in Andersen. This is emphasized in the old woman's additional advice to the young man:

> There are plenty of things to write and tell about, if only you know how. You can draw it out of the plants and the fruits of the earth, ladle it from running and still waters. But you must know how—know how to capture a sunbeam. Just try on my spectacles and put my ear trumpet to your ear, then pray to the Lord, and do stop thinking about yourself!

Here, once again, Andersen addresses the differences or occasional dichotomies between idealism and realism. In general, he fulfills in his writings both of the old woman's demands: he writes texts that can be assigned to romantic idealism, and texts that definitely belong to realism—though never to naturalism, defined as realism turned into a materialistic philosophy of life, according to such French writers as Émile Zola and such Danish writers as Jens Peter Jacobsen.

However, Andersen reaches artistic perfection when he explores *both* tendencies at once: either merging idealism and realism or letting idealism and naturalism clash in his texts; or when he positions himself in the magnetic field between two poles, exploiting the tension whether these are artistic or ideological poles. This is, for instance, the case with his masterpiece "Skyggen" ("The Shadow," 1847), which is indeed a major work in world literature. Here, as Andersen lets "a learned man from the cold countries" write about what is true, good, and beautiful, he articulates not only his own ideal of art but also, in a formula, the values of romanticism. However, the bitter irony of the story is that no one pays attention to these values, and people choose instead to follow the title character, the most demonic character in Danish nineteenth-century literature, a being without substance, whose successful undertakings illustrate how materialism and nihilism have replaced spirituality. Here, nothing is left of the romantic belief that the good-hearted person, such as Elise in "De vilde Svaner" ("The Wild Swans," 1838) or Gerda in "Sneedronningen" ("The Snow Queen," 1845), has nothing to fear from evil: all human efforts are in fact absurd and the learned man is executed!

This is also the main theme in another masterpiece "Historien om en Moder" ("The Story of a Mother," 1848), a tribute to maternal love but also a demonstration of the mercilessness of life. In her endeavors to find her child, whom Death has taken from her, the mother finally

---

4　All translations of the Danish original are from *Tales and Stories by Hans Christian Andersen*, translated and edited by Patricia L. Conroy and Sven H. Rossel. Seattle/London: University of Washington Press, 1980.

realizes that in spite of all her sacrifices she will be left empty-handed. The text concludes as follows:

> And the mother wrung her hands, fell upon her knees, and prayed to the Lord, "Hear me not when I pray for what is not Thy will. Thy will is always best. Hear me not! Hear me not!" And she buried her face in her lap. And Death went with her child into the unknown land.

The reader is thereby confronted with life's absurdity, while what the future will bring remains obscure. We are far from the bright and optimistic atmosphere that permeates Andersen's first fairy tale, "The Tinderbox," which ends with the soldier marrying the princess: "The wedding lasted a week, and the three dogs sat at the table and made eyes at everybody." These texts exemplify how Andersen replaced not only the romantic tale with the realist short story but also the Biedermeier idyll with a modern questioning of traditional concepts.

All of the above artistic and philosophical aspects, including the dormant skepticism and awareness of the relativity of all values, add to the excitement one feels when reading one of Andersen's tales or stories. They add a fascinating touch of modernity to his work. They also form the point of departure for the contributors to the present volume, whose analyses aim to demonstrate how nuanced and complex Andersen's fairy tales are. Tom Lundskær-Nielsen discusses Andersen's unique linguistic genius—his replacement of the frequently rather stilted language of romanticism with that of spoken, colloquial Danish—while Scott Mellor deals with Andersen as a social critic and commentator. In his discussion Mellor includes two of Andersen's lesser-known tales, "Taarnvægteren Ole" ("The Watchman of the Tower," 1859) and "Hjertesorg" ("Grief," 1853), a text that Nate Kramer also takes up in his analysis of Andersen's use of anthropomorphism. Kramer also throws light on other lesser-known texts such as "Det gamle Huus" ("The Old House," 1847), "Loppen og Professoren" ("The Flea and the Professor," 1873), both somewhat overlooked masterpieces that might more accurately be labeled short stories than traditional fairy tales.

Many of the texts discussed in this volume fall outside the canon of Andersen's familiar tales and stories and offer readers a glimpse of Andersen's darker side. While introducing readers to Andersen's lesser-known masterpieces is a worthy end in itself, the essays in this volume also destabilize and correct the tendency toward smoothing out and oversimplifying Andersen's well-known tales, many of which have unfortunately been published as so-called pedagogical retellings found in bookstores' sections for children's literature. Both the essay by Elettra Carbone on gender constructions in "Prindsessen på Ærten" ("The Princess on the Pea," 1835) and "Kejserens nye Klæder" ("The Emperor's New Clothes," 1837) and Karin Sanders' elucidation of Andersen's implicit dialogue with thinkers as diverse as Søren Kierkegaard and Sigmund Freud in "The Shadow" make it clear that some of Andersen's most popular and widely anthologized texts deal with serious issues and can still benefit from new critical approaches. In her readings of the poignant "The Story of Mother" to the ecstatic "Den gamle Egetræs sidste Drøm" ("The Old Oak Tree's Last Dream," 1858), Julie K.

Allen deals with the broad, indeed, universal question, often overlooked in earlier Andersen scholarship, of the role of religion and transcendence in Andersen's works, and Jakob Holm's discussion of the portrait and role of the artist in Andersen's tales "Den flyvende Kuffert" ("The Flying Trunk," 1839), "Pen og Blækhus" ("The Pen and the Inkwell," 1860), and "Flipperne" ("The Collar," 1847) illuminates another of Andersen's major thematic emphases. Jakob Stougaard-Nielsen's discussion of Andersen's depiction of the city focuses on the tale of "Dryaden" ("The Wood Nymph," 1868), a lesser-known but nevertheless seminal text that also attracts the attention of Marianne Stecher, who considers the theme of travel in light of Andersen's fascination with speed and modern technology. By contrast, Nete Schmidt explores how Andersen's tales of travel also relate to the theme of love, using the short story of "Ib og lille Christine" ("Ib and Little Christine," 1855) to set the stage of discussion that culminates in her analysis of the melancholy tale "Under Piletræet" ("Under the Willow Tree," 1853).

The volume concludes with an exploration of various visual representations of Andersen's work and life and their bearing on the reader's understanding of Andersen's tales. Melissa Lucas surveys and explicates the range of illustrations that have accompanied and contributed to the reader's experience of Andersen's tales, and Maren Johnson discusses two cinematic treatments of Andersen's biography from 2003 and 2005, the latter of which, the brilliant *Unge Andersen* (*Young Andersen*), coincided with the bicentennial celebration of the writer's birth. The film received rather negative reviews from Danish critics for its lack of respect toward Andersen, but Johnson fortunately disagrees with this assessment, proving that an outside opinion can add a new and refreshing perspective to already established and generally accepted viewpoints.

The essays that make up the present volume constitute an informative survey of the many innovative approaches and perceptive analyses of today's international Andersen scholarship, drawing on the collective expertise and insights of both established and emerging Andersen teachers and scholars from across the United States and Great Britain. Given its breadth of topics and careful teasing out of meaning, it is a unique contribution to Andersen scholarship that is ideal for facilitating the teaching of Hans Christian Andersen's tales and stories at universities all over the world, as well as offering individual readers the chance to conduct a self-study course in Andersen's tales and stories. While not comprehensive in either its coverage of Andersen's tales or the range of methodological approaches to them, which would require many times the space, this volume conclusively establishes that Andersen's works remain relevant to modern readers and can continue to yield new insights nearly two centuries after their initial publication. In the words of the renowned ballad scholar Sigurd Bernhard Hustvedt, "Though the sheaves have been pretty carefully cleaned from the fields, the threshing is only well begun."[5]

Sven Hakon Rossel
University of Vienna

---

5   Quoted in Sven Hakon Rossel, *Den litterære vise i folketraditionen.* Copenhagen: Akademisk Forlag, 1971, p. 1.

Preface

Like a great many other children across the world, I grew up hearing and reading fairy tales, primarily those told by the Brothers Grimm, Charles Perrault, and Hans Christian Andersen. I loved the tales for the way they seemed to lift the curtain on the magical creatures and forces inhabiting the world around me, demonstrating the power of tables to produce food, boots to span impossible distances, animals to talk, and children to outsmart adults. At some point in my adolescence, I believed that I had outgrown fairy tales and so I set aside my well-loved collections of tales and stories. It wasn't until many years later that I returned to the tales that had played such a prominent role in my childhood, only to discover that their magic was still potent. In fact, rereading these fairy tales as an adult, a parent, and a scholar, I was amazed and delighted to discover that they not only retained the power to ignite my imagination and enthrall me, they were also thick with symbols, cultural clues, linguistic jokes, and meta-textual significance that posed a compelling intellectual challenge.

In connection with my collaboration with Professor Maria Tatar on *The Annotated Hans Christian Andersen* and my preparations for teaching a large undergraduate course on the tales of Hans Christian Andersen at the University of Wisconsin-Madison, I had the opportunity to accept this challenge, immerse myself in the tales of Hans Christian Andersen, and explore the nuances of his literary style and cultural commentary in depth. I was amazed by the wealth of information and meaning within texts that are often dismissed as "just" fairy tales. Yet while a great deal of impressive and important scholarship has been published about Andersen and his works, it can be quite academic and may seem daunting to non-specialists. For this reason, I asked fellow scholars and teachers of Andersen's work from across the United States and Great Britain to collaborate with me on a collection of approaches to Andersen's tales and stories designed specifically for students and other people who happen to love his fairy tales.

The purpose of the book in your hands is, therefore, to enable readers of all ages and backgrounds to take a new, closer look at the tales and stories of Hans Christian Andersen. While Andersen's fairy tales have tremendous value as children's stories and as the basis of many beloved animated films, the essays in this book can help readers discover that fairy tales have much more to offer than just a lively plot, colorful characters, and magic. Andersen's tales and stories are linguistic, artistic, and literary masterpieces that deal with serious matters like sorrow, death, faith, love, and loss. They provide vivid insights into the world in which Andersen lived—the places he visited and people he knew, the social and religious xxii | More Than Just Fairy Tales

changes that European society underwent over the course of his life, and his own hopes and fears. In addition to being translated into more than a hundred languages and published around the world, Andersen's tales have inspired paintings, poetry, music, novels, and films. This book traces the cultural resonance of Andersen's work in a few of these areas, but it cannot—and is not meant to be—exhaustive. Instead, it is my hope that readers will come away from this book equipped with the desire and the skills to explore further on their own, to read Andersen's fairy tales with new eyes, and see how he lifts the curtain for us on both the fanciful and serious aspects of the world and human life.

Julie K. Allen
University of Wisconsin–Madison

Chapter I

The Language of Hans Christian Andersen's Fairy Tales

Tom Lundskær-Nielsen

In the western European fairy-tale tradition, Hans Christian Andersen holds a unique position. In order to understand this, however, it is necessary to take a very brief look at the history of this tradition. Fairy tales have existed from the earliest historical times and in different parts of the world. They were passed on orally from generation to generation, probably changing quite a lot along the way. They were the so-called *folk fairy tales* (cf. German *Volksmärchen*). For obvious reasons, our knowledge about them is rather vague, nor do we know much about the language in which they were told; but although they were transmitted orally and often recited to groups of people, they were by and large aimed at an adult audience.

In more recent times, scholars have distinguished these folk fairy tales from *literary (or artistic) fairy tales* (cf. German *Kunstmärchen*). The term "literary fairy tales" means that at some point, writers started to compose their own tales, thereby creating a new literary genre. However, we should be careful not to overemphasize this difference. First of all, we find examples of written fairy tales or similar stories as far back as in Greek and Roman antiquity; one of the first is that of "Cupid and Psyche," which forms part of Apuleius's narrative, *The Golden Ass*, from the second century AD. Secondly, there was no clear distinction between what we now consider different literary genres, so these tales merged with myths, legends, fables, etc.

Written fairy tales in western Europe emerged in Italy in the 16th and 17th centuries with Straparola in Venice and Basile in Naples. Neither the content nor the language of these tales was for the prudish, and certainly not for children. This was also true of the French fairy tales in the late 17th century, which were written mainly for the court of Louis XIV. The best-known author of fairy tales from this period is Charles Perrault, but quite a few female authors contributed far more tales both then and throughout the 18th century. The genre was given a huge boost with the first European (i.e., French) translation (by Antoine Galland, between 1704–1717) of *1001 Nights* (or *The Arabian Nights*). It is also at this time that the French term *contes de fées* (fairy tales) gained currency.

Up to this point, fairy tales—whether in the oral tradition or as literary works—were thus not aimed at children. The fairy tale was an adult genre, often containing gruesome deeds and/or sexual activity or innuendo, written in a kind of language that was unsuitable for young readers. It was only around the middle of the 18th century that fairy tales began to be created with an audience of children in mind, but even then they were not primarily entertainment; rather, they were part of the educational upbringing of the sons and daughters of the higher and middle classes, instructing them how to behave in polite society.

The pre-Romantic period and the Romantic Age (roughly from 1770–1830) took a keen interest in oral folk traditions. This led to a number of collections of fairy tales, folk stories, and poetry; e.g., by Herder and Musäus in Germany in the late 18th century, but most famously the fairy-tale collections by the Brothers Grimm in the early 19th century. Goethe and the German Romantics (Tieck, Novalis, Hoffmann, et al.) popularized the genre of the *Kunstmärchen*. It appealed to the imagination and to the growing interest in the (national) past, but here too the intended audience was an adult readership and the language of these literary fairy tales reflected that.

In Denmark, where the Romantic principles had been adopted by the cultural elite, fairy tales also featured prominently. In addition to collecting folk fairy tales from different regions, writers such as Adam Oehlenschläger, the most famous Danish Romantic writer, the poet and historical novelist Bernhard Severin Ingemann, and the scholar Christian Molbech translated German fairy tales into Danish and also wrote some of their own. In general, these literary fairy tales follow the traditional patterns for folktales, in both content and language. It was not until the 1830s that a new writer came along, who transformed the notion of what was acceptable in this genre. His name was Hans Christian Andersen.

By the mid-1830s, Andersen was already an established author. He had published literary works in different genres, including a novel, *Improvisatoren* (The Improvisatore; 1835) set in Italy. In some of these rather diverse publications, Andersen uses a style that is in many ways at odds with what was considered "correct language" in the dominant cultural circles in Copenhagen, led by the playwright Johan Ludvig Heiberg. Andersen, with his low social background and lack of proper learning, did not easily fit into this bourgeois establishment, and was not afraid to distance himself from it by flouting its literary conventions. Although he longed to be accepted by its members, he had an acute sense of his own strengths. When it came to the crunch, Andersen's artistic instincts always won the day.

This innate belief in "doing it his own way" is nowhere clearer than in his fairy-tale writing. He knew from the start that he had embarked on something new and rather special. In fact, he had already tested the waters by converting a folk fairy tale into his first tale, "Dödningen" (The Dead Person), and attached it to his volume of poems, published in 1830. It did not find favor with the critics, but it taught Andersen how *not* to write fairy tales. In it, he uses a rather ponderous style with long nature descriptions, but when he takes up fairy tales again five years later, his language has been transformed beyond recognition.

From his extensive correspondence, we have some insight into what had changed, and how Andersen saw his renewed attempts in this genre. For example, in the run-up to the first volume of four fairy tales in 1835, he says in a letter to the Danish poet Ingemann:

> Furthermore, I have begun some "Fairy Tales, Told for Children", and I think I will succeed with them. I have rendered a few of the fairy tales that made me happy to listen to as a child and which I think are not known … . (Bille and Bøgh 1978, 292; my translation).

And then he adds the following significant sentence: "I have written them completely *as I myself would tell them to a child*" (emphasis added).

Even closer to publication, Andersen told the German writer Adelbert von Chamisso (who knew and translated Andersen's tales from the Danish), "In these [the first four tales] I think I have *expressed the childish element in a rather singular way*" (Høybye 1969, 400; my translation and emphasis added). So what Andersen brings to the fairy tales this time around is primarily two new things: *the child's perspective* and *a new kind of language*. In the rest of this chapter, we shall consider some of the characteristics of this "new language."

Generally speaking, what Andersen does from the start is to make his language more "child-friendly," compared with earlier fairy tales, and even with the language he himself used in "The Dead Person." Out went the formal vocabulary, the elaborate constructions, and the long sentences with many subordinate (or dependent) clauses; instead, we find features such as a simple, everyday vocabulary, repetitions, direct speech, modal adverbs, short main clauses, and onomatopoeic (i.e., sound-imitating) expressions, to mention but a few of them. In many places, the reader/listener is addressed directly.

However, this causes a problem for anyone who is unable to read the tales in the original Danish. Andersen's idiosyncratic style is not easy to translate into other languages, and English is a good illustration of this. Some of the more personal or "quirky" elements—e.g., his use of modal adverbs such as *da, jo, nok, vel*, etc. (compare the German near-equivalents *doch, ja, schon, wohl,* etc.)—are mostly untranslatable, but add color and nuances to Andersen's texts, and others (for instance, the paratactic style, see also below) are usually adapted to suit the target language, which diminishes the innovative impact of Andersen's style.[1] In an attempt to adapt Andersen's style to the conventions of the target language, people tend to forget that Andersen's language was highly unconventional and innovative for his time. In this chapter, the English quotations are taken from Erik Christian Haugaard's translation (Andersen 1974), not because it is particularly good, but because, unlike some of the more recent translations, it contains all of Andersen's tales.

Folk tales almost invariably begin with the formulaic, *"Der var engang ..."* (Once upon a time ...), but Andersen uses this opening in only ten of his 156 fairy tales (and not after 1848). This may have been in part to distance himself from the folk fairy tale, but it is more likely that he simply prefers his own individualistic wording. Consider, for example, the beginning of "The Tinderbox" (1835), the very first tale of the first volume: "A soldier came marching down the road: Left ... right! Left ... right! He had a pack on his back and a sword at his side. He had been in the war and he was on his way home" (Andersen 1974, 1). By avoiding the time-honored phrase "once upon a time," this tale feels more contemporary, and we jump straight into the action without any preliminary description, a technique known as *in medias res.* In terms of meaning, there is really no need to add anything to "marching" since we all know what marching sounds like; that is, we adults do. To a child, however, the sound and rhythm of marching is brought home by the imaginary command "Left ... right! Left ... right!," which helps to define the young man as a soldier, even though there is, in fact, no one there to give the order to march.

There are several other onomatopoeic expressions in the text, all of which make the story lively and likely to appeal to children. For instance, when the soldier

Figure 1.1 Harry Clarke's 1916 depiction of the soldier and the witch in "The Tinderbox" is as innovative visually as Andersen's text is narratively.

---

1   For more information on Danish modal adverbs, see Lundskær-Nielsen, T. and Holmes, P. (2010), *Danish: A Comprehensive Grammar.* 2nd ed. London and New York: Routledge, pp. 401–402.

opens the first door down in the tree, he utters an involuntary "Oh!" when he spots the big dog in the room. Or does he? There are no inverted commas around this exclamation (*Uh!* in the original), and it is more logical to see it as an example of free indirect speech where we hear the soldier's reaction via the narrator's voice. This is a device that Andersen perfected in his fairy-tale language. When the soldier opens the second door, an "Aha!" (Danish, *Eia!*) is expressed, but by whom? (2). And the sight of the third dog—the one whose eyes are each as big as the Round Tower in Copenhagen—generates a whole sentence, meaning "Oh, that was hideous!" (but very feebly translated by Haugaard), and again, it is ambiguous who says it.

Onomatopoeic expressions are by no means confined to "The Tinderbox" and other early tales; they are stock-in-trade elements of Andersen's tales. The same can be said of verse lines in many of the tales, such as the Danish-German elegiac couplet from "The Swineherd" (1842): "*Ach, Du lieber Augustin/Alles ist weg, weg, weg* (194); the fairly meaningless and virtually untranslatable verse (since it only exists as a rhyme): "*Snip snap snurre/Basselurre* (Crack and break,/Snap and bend ...) (369) from "The Flax" (1849); or simply the resigned repetition "*Forbi! Forbi!*" (*Gone! Gone!*) that runs like an echo through the ending of "The Fir Tree" (1845) (233, though inexplicably Haugaard calls it "The Pine Tree" and omits the repetition).

This kind of everyday colloquial language, incorporating what many then deemed "unaesthetic" sounds, expressions, and idioms associated with children, was a new departure in fairy tales and widely frowned on by the early critics, who thought it uncivilized and unsuitable for children. Andersen must have been aware that such a reaction was possible, for he seems to preempt it in his first original tale, "Little Ida's Flowers" (1835), where the main perspective has shifted to a child (rather than a soldier, smallholder, or princess, respectively, as in the first three tales). The main theme of the tale is how to introduce a young girl to the concept of death. The approach taken by the student is to appeal to the imagination and transfer the "problem" to the dying flowers, as he tells Ida that the flowers "have been dancing all night and that is why they look so tired and hang their heads" (22). His adversary, the literal-minded, bad-tempered counselor (a personified caricature of the Enlightenment), rejects "*den dumme Phantasie*" (the stupid imagination, though Haugaard leaves out the entire phrase) as something that is harmful to children, but it is the student's insight into child psychology that enables him to persuade Ida to accept the flowers' present death (and resurrection the following

Figure 1.2 "Little Ida's Flowers" in an 1866 engraving by the Dalziel brothers.

year). The reason for this outcome is that the student can tap into the child's way of thinking and her fertile imagination. Through his use of imagery, he is thus able to convince her of an aspect of life that the counselor can neither comprehend nor formulate. This creates a natural bond between them, and gives her confidence in the student.

The first two pages or so of the tale, up to the counselor's intervention, consists almost entirely of a dialogue between Ida and the student, with the majority of the lines spoken by the student. Here, the student, as well as using words and idioms that Ida can understand and appreciate, also employs a device that was to become the hallmark of Andersen's style: viz., a distinctly paratactic syntax. This usually takes the form of long sentences—"sentence" is used here in the sense of what is written between two full stops—but very few subordinate clauses. Instead of having a linking subordinate conjunction, we find main clause heaped upon main clause, separated from the previous one merely by a comma or a semicolon, or by a coordinating conjunction such as *and, but,* or *for.* This adds urgency and almost breathless speed to the reading (or listening) process, and marks the style as simple, immediate, catching, and alive: something that a child will appreciate.

We can illustrate this style with the student's account of butterflies, which, in a direct translation, would go something like this:

> I'm sure you have seen beautiful butterflies, red, yellow and white ones, they look almost like flowers, and so they once were; they jumped off the stem high into the air and then flapped the leaves as if they were small wings, and then they flew, and because they were so good at moving upwards, they were even allowed to fly in the daytime; they didn't have to go home and sit quietly on the stem, and then the leaves became real wings in the end. (My translation, cf. Andersen 2003, 101)

You can really only read this sequence of clauses quickly and fluently. However, translations of this passage into English are often chopped up into separate sentences and thus lose this all-important fluency. Compare this passage with Haugaard's translation below, which, in addition, treats some of the details in a rather cavalier fashion. Then judge for yourself which version is more likely to appeal to a child.

> You have seen butterflies. Don't they look like yellow, red, and white flowers? That is exactly what they were once. They are flowers who have jumped off their stems and have learned to fly with their petals; and when they first get a taste for it, they never return to their stems, and their little petals become real wings. (Andersen 1974, 23)

The child's perspective can also be seen in the many similes and explanations, which are completely superfluous for adult readers. Among the countless examples of this, take, for instance, the beginning of "The Little Mermaid" (1837):

> Far, far from land, where the waters are as blue as the petals of the cornflower and as clear as glass, there, where no anchor can reach the bottom, live the mer-people. So

deep is this part of the sea that you would have to pile many church towers on top of each other before one of them emerged above the surface. (57)

The words "blue" and "clear" need no further specification for adults, but here they are compared with well-known phenomena from everyday life (cornflower petals and glass), while the depth of the ocean is measured by means of the length of an anchor cable and the combined height of many church towers; all things that are familiar to children. A little later we are told that down in the deep where "the most wondrous trees and plants" grow, "all the fishes, big and small, flit in and out between the branches, just like the birds up here on earth" (my translation). The adverb phrase "up here" is symptomatic of the viewpoint not only of humans, but of children in particular, as is the comparison between fishes and birds.

Another feature of child-oriented language is the direct address by the narrator, especially in preparing the reader/listener for what is to come. The narrator often intrudes in the narration to draw attention to the listening activity; hence, the numerous instances of the verb *to hear*. It appears throughout his fairy-tale production right from the start in "The Tinderbox," when the soldier, languishing in the prison, gets his tinderbox back

Figure 1.3 "The Little Mermaid" by Honor C. Appleton in 1922 captures the nuances of color that Andersen describes in the text.

and—well, what then? Or as Andersen puts it, "And now you shall *hear* what happened after that!" (6; emphasis added). In "Little Claus and Big Claus" (1835), we are told at the end of the first paragraph, "Now let's *hear* what happened to two of them because that's a real story!" (8; emphasis added), and in "The Snow Queen" (1845)—at the end of the first story—we read, "And now you shall *hear* about them" (6; emphasis added). Throughout the tales there are many variations of this.

A tale may open with a rhetorical question, as, for example, in "The Shepherdess and the Chimney Sweep" (1845) with its opening lines: "Have you ever seen a really old cabinet, the kind whose wood is dark from age and that doesn't have a spot on it that isn't carved, so that it looks like a mass of vines and twirls?" (297), which serve the purpose of catching the attention of the (child) listener from the start. In fact, the need to tell the story at all may be queried in this way, as in "The Old Street Lamp" (1847), which begins with the question, "Have you ever heard the story of the old street lamp?" (313), although the assumption is obviously that the answer will be in the negative.

There is also wide variation in the ways that the narrator may choose to address the reader, particularly the young listener. For example, at the beginning of "The Daisy" (1838), the narrator states that, "there once was a country house with a beautiful garden and a white fence around it" (108), and draws the listener in by appealing to an air of familiarity when he adds, "you yourself have surely already seen it," but sadly, this intimate comment has been cut by Haugaard.

It is, of course, impossible in so short a space to deal with more than a limited number of language elements in the fairy tales, and so far we have concentrated on some of the more obvious ones. However, a few more must be mentioned briefly. One of these concerns the "development" in Andersen's style over the nearly four decades (1835–1872) that he composed his fairy tales. On the one hand, there is no doubt that some of the later ones are more descriptive, especially the "stories," as he started calling them from the 1850s on (e.g., "A Story from the Dunes," 1860), though at the same time, he introduces new symbolic devices such as the sounds of the wind in "What the Wind Told about Valdemar Daae and His Daughters" (1859). On the other hand, certain linguistic and stylistic elements can be found throughout the tales, e.g., the simple vocabulary, the paratactic style, the direct address to the reader/listener, etc. If this demonstrates the impossibility of generalizing about Andersen's language, there is another layer to it as well: Andersen's "simplistic style" is just as artistic (and so, in a sense, artificial) as that of other writers of *Kunstmärchen*.

We should not forget either that although many of the texts contain features that appeal particularly to children, the fairy tales were not written *solely* for this audience. Andersen is keen to point out that they are intended for both children and adults. After 1842, he deliberately dropped the subtitle "Told for Children" because he thought that it had been misunderstood, and in the preface to the first collected edition of his *Fairy Tales and Stories* (1862), he managed to include in one sentence three of the key elements that make his tales unique by saying, "In style one ought to hear the narrator; these stories were made to suggest oral delivery; they were told for children but their elders should also enjoy listening to them" (Andersen 1862, my translation). So here we have: (a) the visibility of the narrator; (b) the colloquial style of the spoken language; and (c) the double audience which he always

Figure 1.4 Lorenz Frølich's 1867 illustration of "What the Wind Told of Valdemar Daae."

had in mind. This goes a long way toward explaining how even today the tales can be read and understood at different levels.

The final aspect to mention here is humor. Danes generally regard Andersen as a humorous writer, but foreign readers who have read him in translation tend to disagree. Why? The most obvious answer is that this feature is difficult to convey in the translations, partly for the reasons given above. For Andersen himself, it was clearly an important ingredient, for as late as two months before his death on 4 August 1875, he notes in his diary, "The naïve elements were only part of my fairy tales ... , the humor was actually the salt in them" (my translation, cf. Andersen 2003, 20). The humor manifests itself in the tales in numerable ways which we cannot go into here, but much of it is due to the oblique angle from which Andersen views life and all the creatures in it and their interactions with each other. After all, animals, trees, flowers, artifacts, etc., can think and even talk, at least among themselves, which leads to incongruous and droll situations where some items act in accordance with their nature and others do not, without there being any particular logic to it. In this way, Andersen can say what is often inexpressible in any other context, and at the same time preserve a degree of superficial innocence, which is yet another example of his ability to communicate in a multilayered fashion to different audiences.

To sum up, Andersen broke new ground within the fairy-tale genre right from his earliest collection in 1835, and one of the main reasons for this is his use of language. In this "new" fairy-tale language, there are many typical child-oriented features. Some of these appear more frequently in the early tales, but they are found throughout the fairy-tale production. Moreover, the consistent colloquial style, typified by simplicity, frequent use of dialogue, free indirect speech, and paratactic syntax, helps to enliven the text and appeal to children. All this is part and parcel of Andersen's particular way of writing fairy tales and is used to reach his double audience of children and adults alike, but this in turn is both an artistic and subversive way of deviating from the norms of the genre. We can therefore conclude by saying that, especially in his early fairy tales, an important element of the novelty in Andersen's approach was that he wrote not just *for* children but *to* children—as well as for adults—and at the time, that was something revolutionary in the fairy-tale genre.

Works Cited

Andersen, H.C. (1862). *H. C. Andersens Eventyr og Historier*. Vol. 1 Copenhagen: C.A. Reitzel.

Andersen, H. C. (2003). *H. C. Andersens samlede værker*. Vol. 1, edited by Klaus P. Mortensen, Det Danske Sprog- og Litteraturselskab. Copenhagen: Gyldendal.

Andersen, H.C. (1974). *The Complete Fairy Tales and Stories*, translated by Erik Christian Haugaard. London: Victor Gollancz.

Bille, C., and Bøgh, N., eds. (1978). *Breve fra Hans Christian Andersen*. Vol. 1. Copenhagen: C. A. Reitzel.

Høybye, P. (1969). "Chamisso, H. C. Andersen og andre danskere." *Anderseniana* 1969: 400.

Lundskær-Nielsen, T., and Holmes, P. (2010). *Danish: A Comprehensive Grammar*. 2nd ed. London and New York: Routledge.

Chapter II

Opinionated Houses and Companionable Fleas

Anthropomorphism in the Fairy Tales of Hans Christian Andersen

Nate Kramer

One of my newfound favorites of Andersen's fairy tales is "Grief." I've usually passed over the tale in favor of more popular ones such as "The Nightingale" or "The Story of a Mother," "The Bell," or "The Shadow," but there is something to the tale with its disarming simplicity and then sudden and surprising shift in perspective at the conclusion. The story is a simple one about a dog that has died and whose grave has now become an exhibit to the delight of the neighborhood children. One of the boys has taken to charging a button for anyone who would like to see the burial site. Granted, not much in the way of an exciting plot. However, in the very last paragraph, we arrive at the true source of the titular grief through a surprising twist. Given the opening of the tale, we might have assumed it would be the sadness of the woman who owned the dog. Or we might assume that the children who had played with the dog and dressed it up as

Figure 2.1 Alfred Walter Bayes' engraving for "Grief": "Waiting to see Puggie's Grave," (1866).

a bridesmaid on occasion would be the source of grief. The passing of the dog and its burial, as well as the expected effects it would have on its owner and the children, have nothing to do with the grief named in the title. Rather, the source of sorrow is a little girl—"although dressed in rags she was lovely" (Andersen 1983, 415)—who doesn't own a button to pay the price of admission to the dog's grave. What seemingly started out as a tale focused on the passing of a poor little dog quickly turns into social commentary about the pain and sadness of poverty and deprivation.

While such social commentary is certainly worthy of exploration, and Andersen's tales often engage this socioeconomic dimension, as Scott Mellor documents in his chapter in this volume, this tale always makes me think not just of the beautiful and destitute little girl, but of the dog, its owner, and the children who played with it for all those years. What happened to them? Where is their grief, and why does Andersen not show it? What of the dog's own perspective, now become a mere attraction for those who can pay? While these may appear to be silly questions, unanswerable in any definitive way by the tale itself, I believe that Andersen fully intended for the reader to ask them. In fact, the tension in the difference between the expectations subtly established in the first part of the tale and the twist in the end depends precisely on the reader asking such questions. I think Andersen wants us to feel for the dog, to engage the perspective not just of the dog, but also of the others who cared for and played with the dog, if only to overturn that perspective in the end.

There is little in the tale and its narratological sleight of hand that could be strictly called anthropomorphism, the topic that will concern us in this chapter. The tale does, however, capture what I take to be the crucial aspect of the anthropomorphic: this idea of perspective, of shifting and alternating positions from which to view ourselves as well as the world. Anthropomorphism is usually thought of as endowing nonhuman creatures and objects with human attributes and characteristics, but anthropomorphism, especially the way we think of it today, is also about "ecology"—understood as the relationship between things and texts as either explicitly or implicitly establishing hierarchies and orders of relationships between things.

Consider the closing paragraph of "Grief": "Now that was grief, a sorrow as sharp as a grownup's can be! We saw it from above; and the little girl's sorrow—like many of our own—was laughable when seen from above" (415). Here, the narrator reveals the intent behind the narratological choices. As readers, we have not sympathized with the little girl until just before this statement, since we've only been introduced to her in the very end. We therefore may well find her sadness trivial and simple. Our sympathies lie rather with the dog and with the owner and the children because we have followed them from the very beginning of the tale. This difference in perception, this perspective, as our narrator calls it, "from above," provides a further context for the tale. "Grief" is no longer about sadness due to loss (whether the experience of poverty or the passing of a pet), but the problems of occupying perspectives outside of and beyond on our own. What does the world look like outside of our own experience of it? How do others think and feel? What is their experience? Is it possible to imagine another's view, or am I condemned to a solipsism that fails to take account of the other? What is the experience of other human beings? Or even a dog, for that matter? I take "Grief" to be a compelling illustration of the ecological as well as the anthropomorphic, insofar as it insists on the possibility of mutually exclusive positions and the problems of seeing from these other positions.

If "Grief" lacks the basic features of anthropomorphism, it does raise the question of our relationship to the animal and thus, for our purposes, points us toward the ubiquitous anthropomorphism in Andersen's oeuvre. Andersen's fairy-tale world is full of animated creatures and objects that often think and feel as human beings, but are clearly not human. A quick look at the list of Andersen's tales in the Erik Haugaard translation reveals not only mermaids, trees, flowers, storks, dung beetles, ducklings, and nightingales who are given human characteristics, but also pens and inkwells, tea kettles, needles, shirt collars, houses, and what are called "stampers" (heavy machines used to set cobblestones firmly in place). Thus, the ascription of human attributes and characteristics applies not just to animals, but anything other than human beings, to any nonhuman creature and object, though it will be the human/animal divide that will structure much of the discussion below since it has dictated much of the critical discussion surrounding anthropomorphism.

Anthropomorphism has a long history. We have been giving rocks, plants, trees, and just about anything else human features for quite some time. Adam Horowitz (2007) notes that some of the earliest occurrences of anthropomorphism can be found in Paleolithic art, some forty thousand years ago (60). Religious scholars contend that all religious systems involve anthropomorphism in one form or another. In fact, aside from its use in fables and fairy tales, anthropomorphism is most often discussed in the context of ascribing human form and attributes to a deity. Anthropomorphism as a literary device, often called "personification," is quite ancient as well. The tales of Aesop, a seventh-century Greek fabulist, are an early example of the use of personification and anthropomorphism, and Aesop was one of the most popular storytellers to do this.[1] Fairy tales also contain their fair share of anthropomorphism, including the earliest collections, those of the French 17th-century writer Charles Perrault and the 19th-century Brothers Grimm, which feature talking animals and birds, for example.

The crucial question for our purposes is why. Why do human beings use personification and anthropomorphism, and for what end? Horowitz claims that "anthropomorphizing is a natural human tendency, thought to be the result of a perceptual system designed to find order in a complex world. Contemporary humans tend, perhaps like our forebears, to interpret a landscape entirely free of human presence as thick with human faces: on a slab of rock, in the gnarl of a tree knot, in the waxing moon, in a pendulous flower" (60). In short, we have a tendency to see ourselves everywhere. The purpose of such a tendency is to "find order in a complex world." By endowing nonhuman creatures and objects with human intention, motivations, thoughts, and feelings, we explain events and occurrences that do not make sense to us. The problem, however, is that in doing so, anthropomorphism risks being "premature or incomplete, and at worst dangerously misleading," because it fails to account for the possibility that the world and the nonhuman objects do not think and feel as humans do. Anthropomorphism thus becomes, according to John Simons (2002), "displaced metaphors for the human" (6). Simons's ultimate point is that animals become mere metaphors and no longer real in such anthropomorphism, but his concerns echo a broader criticism about how human beings treat and respond to the natural world and the animals in it, an issue raised by various scientists, including ecologists and eco-critics. The core problem here may not only be epistemological, though. Timothy Clark (2011) points out "the inherently anthropocentric nature of human language, projecting as it does a world usually understood according to our own scale, dimensions, interests and desires" (192). Clark raises here the problem of the anthropocentric nature not only of human language, but of potentially all modes of representing the nonhuman world (visual, musical, etc.).

If anthropocentrism appears to be an insurmountable obstacle, Clark suggests a way out of the dead end. "Language that may seem problematically figurative or 'merely anthropomorphic' can also acquire provocative value as a way of doing justice to the agency of the nonhuman" (192). In fact, Clark suggests that anthropomorphism itself paradoxically provides just such a decentering impulse: "The issue of 'anthropomorphism,' positioned on the hazy borderlines between human and non-human, can become a powerful tool for questioning the complacency of dominant human self-conceptions" (192). If we couple Simons's notion of anthropomorphism as displaced metaphors with Clark's conception of anthropomorphism as a tool for questioning human complacency, we may well escape (though we will have to be careful) the reductive and simplistic attitudes that often plague anthropomorphism. Indeed, metaphors offer powerful ways of understanding ourselves and our experience of the world around us. Rather than seeing metaphors as debased currency, as secondary—as

---

1   The actual existence of Aesop, as well as his authoring the fables he is known for, is in some doubt. However, since the 5th century, a coherent picture of Aesop as the author of the fables appeared, and this view has persisted throughout the centuries.

Plato did—we must recognize that metaphors enable us to think and imagine in ways that we never could if we didn't have them. What is it "like" to be another person, a woman, a man, a dog, a tree, a member of the African Igbo tribe, a flower? In the following readings of two of Andersen's tales, I would like to pay attention to how such anthropocentrism is used to trouble our human complacency and challenge certain views we might have of ourselves or of the nonhuman, by seeing them from both the inside and the outside.

If we are to think of anthropomorphism in Andersen's tales as a tool for questioning such complacency, it is imperative that we think about not only how the nonhuman and the human are represented, but how the nonhuman is essential for understanding the human. In his book, *Picturing the Beast*, Steven Baker (1993) suggests the stakes of such representation by asking how we depict or represent the animal in popular culture. He asks, "why is it that our ideas of the animal—perhaps more than any other set of ideas—are the ones which enable us to frame and express ideas about human identity?" (6). This question will set the stage for what follows. Indeed, this is the significance of anthropomorphism as I see it in Andersen's tales: Andersen's notion of the animal (as well as the other nonhuman objects in his fictional world) helps to construct what I take to be at the center of Andersen's fairy-tale universe: the human being and the question of what it means to be human.

"The Old House" (1847)

"The Old House" was first published in 1847 shortly before Christmas and, interestingly enough, in English translation, due to concerns about unauthorized republication. The tale itself is about the passage of time and what gets lost and forgotten in the process (though it is also about a good deal more, as we shall see). To illustrate the changes that take place as time marches on, Andersen focuses our attention on a house, an old house, that seems the worse for wear. Our first indication of anthropomorphism is found in the second paragraph, where the narrator tells us, speaking of the houses that surround the old house:

> It was quite reasonable that they should feel themselves superior to the old house. Had they been able

Figure 2.2 "The Old House," depicted by Hans Tegner in an edition of Andersen's tales from 1900.

to speak they probably would have said, "How long are we to tolerate that old ruin? Bow windows are out of fashion and, besides, they obstruct our view. It must believe itself to be a castle, judging from the size of the steps leading up to the entrance, and that iron railing makes one think of funerals; not to speak of the brass knobs. It's embarrassing!" (Andersen 1983, 346)

That houses should have a sense of superiority among their peers is not something that might have occurred to most of us, let alone that they should have opinions about views and fashion and even what funerals are, as well as what is socially acceptable or not. What is surprising here is not that houses have feelings or sensibilities, but that these houses have *our* feelings and sensibilities. Often, the function of anthropomorphism isn't to imagine what it would be like to be something other than our human selves, but to tell us something about the way we think and feel as human beings.

Though the house is judged to be outdated and out of fashion by the others, a little boy who lives across the street sees something else in the house. The boy is fascinated by the decrepit old house. The house is a virtual window into a past that the boy will never know, but can imagine and recreate in his mind:

> When he looked at the walls of the old house, with its cracks and bare spots where the mortar had fallen off, he could imagine how the street once had looked: in olden times, when all the houses had had broad steps leading up to the doors, and bay windows, and gables with tall pointed roofs. He could see the soldiers marching through the streets armed with halberds. Oh, he found the old house worth looking at and dreaming about. (347)

The boy's reaction is typical of many of Andersen's tales, in which someone or something recognizes value in what others perceive as insignificant or irrelevant. While the above is not a case of anthropomorphism per se, as readers, we become aware of a developing relationship with the house as if it were something human, or at least something that can think and feel and even reciprocate.

In the old house lives an old man whom the boy befriends. One day, the boy sends one of his two tin soldiers to the old man, thus paving the way for a visit to the house and to the old man. Upon the boy's visit, we encounter more anthropomorphism, as we look at the house through his eyes.

> The little carved trumpeters in the oak doorway seemed to be blowing especially hard on their instruments, for their cheeks were all puffed up. It was a fanfare! "Tra ... tra ... trattalala! The boy is coming! Tra ... tra ... trattalala!" ... All the walls were covered with paintings portraying ladies in long silk gowns and knights in armor. The boy thought that he could hear the silk gowns rustle and the armor clang ... one could

almost hear the play saying: "The breeze has caressed me and the sun has kissed me and promised me a flower next Sunday, a little flower next Sunday." (347–48)

One might note here the way the anthropomorphism flits back and forth between the boy's imagining the house announcing his arrival and a more literal anthropomorphism, in which the house actually does speak. "In the room were high-backed armchairs with carvings all over them. 'Sit down, sit down!' they cried. And when you sat down in them they mumbled. 'Ugh, how it cracks inside me! I think I got rheumatism like the old cabinet. Ugh, how it creaks and cracks'" (348).

While the boy's relationship to the old house and the man who lives in it takes center stage, especially the boy's rather sentimental reaction to them, the addition of an anthropomorphized tin soldier creates a critical tension in the narrative. In fact, the second part of the tale is very much the story of the tin solider left behind at the house by the little boy. Though the tin soldier is owned by the boy, it does not share the boy's enthusiasm for either the old house or the old man, and thus provides an important contrast to the boy's own feelings.[2] The tin soldier complains about being left at the old house: "'But I can't stand it here!' wailed the tin soldier, who was standing on the lid of a chest. 'It is so lonely and sad here; once you have lived with a family one cannot get accustomed to being alone. I can't stand it! The days are ever so long and the evenings feel even longer" (349). Where the boy is enamored of "all the old thoughts and dreams [that] come to visit," the tin soldier sees and hears none of them, nor does he want to. This introduces a critical ambiguity into the narrative as to how we are to think of the past and our relationship to it. If the boy finds the past exciting and fascinating, the tin soldier finds the past inhibiting and indeed confining, like a prison. "'I have wept tin tears! It is much too mournful and sad here. Please, let me go to the wars and lose my arms and legs, that at least will be a change. I can't stand it, for I know what it is like to have old thoughts and old memories come visiting. Mine have been here and that is not amusing'" (350).

Andersen can sometimes be heavy-handed, but many of his better tales stop short of telling readers how to think about a character or an event in his stories. Such a move is Andersen's own contribution to the often moralizing and pedagogical fables and fairy tales that Andersen was influenced by and would have been familiar with. In "The Old House," we also find a moral, but it is not what we might expect. In the last paragraph of the story, the little boy, now grown, has purchased the property on which the old house stood, though the house itself no longer remains.[3] With the loss of the old house and the old man who has died, the memories of them and the power they had on the young boy seem to have faded

---

2   If we were to psychologize a little further, we might even say that the tin soldier represents the alter ego of the boy. Significantly, the tin soldier is left at the old house, much to its dismay, as if the little boy wishes to leave a part of himself in the old house.

3   We may wonder at the man's purchase of the property across the street from where he grew up and the place where the old house stood. As in footnote 2, I will not be arguing a psychological motivation for this, but a close reading of the tale warrants it.

as well. That is, until one day the man's wife finds the forgotten tin soldier in the garden along with a piece of leather that used to cover the walls of the old house. The woman shows her husband the tin soldier, upon which the man tells the story we have just been rehearsing. Moved by the tale, the man's wife wipes off the tin solider, intending to keep him "so that I shall not forget the story you have told me" (352). The tin soldier is also glad to have been found and "not forgotten," but in one last nod toward anthropomorphism, the scrap of leather wall covering that has also been found comments: "Gilding fades all too fast/But leather, that is meant to last." Here is the moral mentioned above; as readers we may be prepared for it. But Andersen undermines the moral in the very last sentence. The tin solider—not the leather wallpaper—gets the last word in the tale by disagreeing with the declared moral. We are simply and straightforwardly informed that "the tin soldier did not believe that" (353). This is the concluding sentence of the tale.

We are left with these two differing perspectives on time and change. Note that both of these perspectives belong to anthropomorphized objects, not the little boy whom we may well have expected to have the last word. In giving the story over to the tin soldier and the wallpaper, the perspective of the little boy has become rather insignificant, though we followed him for much of the story. In fact, his fascination with the old house seems to have been replaced by adult concerns and worries in the conclusion. He has left the imaginative world of his youth behind and is no longer interested in those experiences, or interested in them now only as memories of a forgotten past. The tin soldier and the wallpaper, however, are vestiges of this past. The tin soldier is as entrenched as ever in his view that things don't last, that change is imminent, and that holding on to the past only brings pain and loneliness. The wallpaper, on the other hand, rejects such a view and insists that it is only the superficial (gilding) that changes, and that real quality (leather) lasts. By giving over the conclusion to these two nonhuman characters that express very human perspectives on time and change, we gain insight into the validity of each view. This is to say that Andersen employs anthropomorphism to provide various perspectives on the passage of time that humans themselves would not necessarily be able to have in and of themselves. Anthropomorphizing the house and its contents in this way gives us a different insight into the temporal dimensions of human experience. They, too, are living, breathing, feeling things. They, too, mark the passage of time.

"The Professor and the Flea" (1873)

"The Professor and the Flea" is a rather late tale among Andersen's works and provides what at first glance is a rather entertaining—if curious—adventure, in which a professor and a flea journey to a land of cannibals, are imprisoned for a time, and then make a daring escape. Andersen was inspired by a number of sources, including French politician Léon Gambetta's spectacular escape from Paris in a hot-air balloon in 1870, the meeting of famed British naturalist David Livingstone and American journalist Henry Morton Stanley in the wilds of

Africa in 1871, and Jules Verne's tale of a Dr. Ferguson and his servant Joe, who traveled to Africa in a balloon.[4] Andersen's tale begins with the tragic death of the professor's father in a harrowing balloon accident, an accident from which the professor as a young man had barely escaped. While this beginning appears to be irrelevant for much of the tale, the young man's one desire is to buy a balloon and to "ascend into the sky with his wife" (Andersen 1983, 1022). This dream is eventually fulfilled at the conclusion of the tale, with the professor and the flea (and not the wife!) making their escape from the land of the cannibals in a balloon of his own construction. On closer inspection, however, the tale suggests a more complex interweaving of plot elements that bear not simply on an adventure story, but really on the question of what it means to be a human being, especially as those elements converge on the relationship between the animal and the human.

Our first encounter with the flea occurs when another tragedy strikes the professor. This time, the professor's wife abandons him, ostensibly because the living they eke out as a traveling circus act and magic show is much too small. His wife's departure is too much for the professor to take, and he suffers from what could only be described as a mental breakdown. His one consolation is the flea that his wife has left him: "He had inherited the animal from his wife and therefore was fond of it. He trained the flea, taught it the art of dexterity: how to present arms and to shoot off a cannon; the latter was very small" (1023). In a careful reading of the tale, the flea becomes not just a memory of the professor's departed wife, but indeed a vestige of, and eventually a substitute for, his wife.[5] Andersen's narrator draws an even stronger connection between the flea and the human being when he adds that "the professor was proud of the flea and the flea was proud of himself. After all, he had human blood in his stomach, if not in his veins. He had visited the grand capitals of Europe and performed before kings and queens, at least that was what was printed in the playbill and the newspapers. He knew he was famous and could support a professor—or a whole family if he had one" (1023). At this point in the tale, which is still quite early, the story seems to gesture in a different direction from which it began. Why this equation of the flea with the human? On the one hand, this may simply be a comical aside playing on the very real appetite of the flea for human blood, a problem that still besets humanity in some corners of the world, though not as widely it used to. On the other hand, the narrator pursues this proximity of the flea to the human further and in much more anthropomorphic terms. The flea is a traveler and has toured Europe, not just along with the professor, but apparently also as an individual. Stranger still, the flea "knows" he is famous and can "support" a professor or a family. If we are not only observant but critical, we might even ask why it is *these* features that make the flea almost human. And further, what is it exactly that the narrator seems to be saying about human beings in such a selection? Is it the blood in our veins that makes

---

4   See the commentary in Det Danske Sprog- og Litteraturselskab's collection of Andersen's fairytales.
5   This is not the place to deal with a more Freudian reading of the tale, but one can't help think about the events of the tale in light of the death of the father and this desire to ascend into the sky once more, but now with a wife. If the wife becomes a substitute for the lost father, it would appear that the flea becomes a substitute for the lost wife.

us human? The desire to travel and explore? Is it the associations we have, a family, and the support of the same?

The association between humans and fleas is certainly not Andersen's invention alone. Fleas and humans have lived side by side for much of human history; in fact, fleas have influenced a great deal of that history. Eric Chaline (2011) has called the flea, "the animal that has most changed the course of history (apart from ourselves, of course). ... In the past 1200 years, the oriental rat flea has been responsible for three pandemics that have killed hundreds of millions, and each time set human civilization on a new course" (204). The flea is known, for example, to be one of the primary vectors for spreading the Black Death, or bubonic plague, beginning in and around Constantinople in 1347. We don't know what kind of flea Andersen is using in his tale, nor is it relevant. What is relevant is that the history of humans has long been tied in fundamental ways to the flea, whether through pandemics or as the often simple tiny annoyances they usually are. The anthropomorphizing of the flea that Andersen's narrator carries out in the tale alludes to this common history as it also begins to interrogate the dividing line between human and animal and the interdependence of species.

In conjunction with the history of humans and fleas, we should mention the flea circus that is alluded to in the tale as well. In the story, the professor "trained the flea, taught it the art of dexterity: how to present arms and to shoot off a cannon; the latter was very small" (Andersen 1983, 1023). This particular anthropomorphization of the flea also has its own history. Flea circuses were quite common during the 19th century, and fleas would be trained to perform all sorts of rather "human" activities. Some walked tightropes and others juggled. Because of their strong hind legs (fleas can jump many times their size and pull objects many times their weight), fleas would also power bicycles and pull minute carriages and hearses. There are records of nuns in Mexico even dressing fleas to look like people.[6] The above not only underscores the historical

Figure 2.3 This 1919 photograph from a Seattle curio shop illustrates the popularity of dressed-up fleas and flea circuses.

6   See Brendan Lehane's entertaining *The Compleat Flea* for more information on fleas and their history. I have consulted the chapter titled "Performing Fleas" for the section above.

connection of the flea to the human, but also the rather strange contiguity and proximity of the flea and the human as such.

If we take the approach that Andersen's tale is interested in exploring the relationship between the professor and the flea in terms of human companionship and not only as the relationship between owner and pet, the tale takes an important turn when the professor and the flea decide to travel to the "lands of the savages" (1022).[7] While as citizens of the 21st century we should object to such a very 19th-century designation of what is ostensibly Africa or the Pacific Islands, this encounter with the "savage," or what I will call the subhuman, arrives precisely here in the context of the relationship between the human and the flea and the human/animal–nonhuman divide.[8] In invoking the subhuman, Andersen's narrator thus inflects the professor and flea relationship and further probes what it means to be human via its distinction from what is not human. In the land of the savages, the professor and the flea are met by a princess who rules the country: "She had overthrown her own parents, for though she was only eight years old she had a will of her own and was marvelously charming and naughty" (1023). The princess becomes enamored of the flea's circus tricks and falls in love with it. The narrator tells us that, "as love can make a civilized man into a savage, imagine what it can do to one who is already a savage" (1023–24). The princess's parents, seemingly disappointed in the marriage choice of their daughter, make the concession that, "We shall have to make [the flea] into a human first. 'You leave that to me, old man,' she answered, and that was not a very nice way to speak to her own father, but she was a savage" (1024).

The domestic comedy unfolding in the above is no doubt familiar to us from literature, film and television, but important for our purposes is the framing of this encounter in terms of anthropomorphism. This is not only about an ill-matched love affair, but the question of what a human being is, filtered through the question of the animal and the subhuman. The boundaries separating each appear to be rather fluid in the tale, insofar as love can make a civilized human being into a savage and the parents' insistence that the flea be transformed into a human before the wedding. This transformation, as well as the wedding, happens simply by the professor putting the flea in the princess's hand and the princess declaring, "'Now you are a human being.' You shall reign together with me, but you will have to obey or I shall kill you and eat the professor'" (1024). That the princess simply declares the flea to be a human being should give us readers pause. What does it mean to simply claim the flea as a human being, especially given the circumstances? We may even pursue this line of questioning implicit in the tale further: What does it mean to be a human being at all when someone can simply declare a flea to be one? What really is the difference between the flea

---

7 One might consider the distinction I've set up here between a relationship of real "human companionship" and "owner and pet" a problematic one, to say the least. In fact, one of the underlying goals of this paper is to complicate such differences.
8 We might consider the argument put forward by various philosophers regarding what is known as "species-ism." The logic of species-ism rests on the ability to distinguish in some absolute sense the differences between species. Such distinctions, according to Peter Singer, are put forward to justify not only treatment of animals but, in the past, racism.

and the professor, or the princess for that matter? Without probing these questions any further, the tale ends with the professor and the flea finally escaping the princess and the land of the savages, rising high into the clouds in a balloon.

Andersen never really answers any of the questions raised in the tale. In fact, Andersen seems to be content simply to raise such questions. In some ways, this is the tale's charm. Still, one can't help but think about these questions, insofar as much of the tale hinges on them. In fact, in many of Andersen's tales involving anthropomorphism, this difference between the human and the animal or the human and the nonhuman is constantly being explored, but never resolved. We shouldn't be dismayed that these questions are asked and not answered. Often, the task of literature is to encourage us to reflect on these and other issues because they have no answer in any definitive sense. Insofar as Andersen's tales are about what it means to be a human being, even when they seem to be discussing an animal, a monster, or some inanimate object, the use of anthropomorphism shakes us out of our complacency and strengthens our capacity to reflect on who we are.

Works Cited

Andersen, H.C. (1983). *The Complete Fairy Tales and Stories*, translated by Erik Christian Haugaard. New York: Anchor Books.

Andersen, H.C. (1986). [1873] "Loppen og Professoren." In *H. C. Andersens eventyr*, Vol. 7. Det Danske Sprog- og Litteraturselskab. Copenhagen: C. A. Reitzels Forlag.

Auden, W. H. (1973). "Grimm and Andersen." In *Forewords and Afterwords*. New York: Random House.

Baker, S. (1993). *Picturing the Beast: Animals, Identity and Representation*. Manchester and New York: Manchester UP.

Chaline, E. (2011). *Fifty Animals That Changed the Course of History*. Buffalo: Firefly Books.

Clark, T. (2011). *The Cambridge Introduction to Literature and the Environment*. Cambridge: Cambridge UP.

Garrard, G. (2004). *Ecocriticism*. London and New York: Routledge.

Horowitz, A. (2007). "Anthropomorphism." In *Encyclopedia of Human-Animal Relationships*, edited by M. Bekoff, 60-66. Westport, CT: Greenwood Publishing Group.

Lehane, B. (1969). *The Compleat Flea*. London: John Murray.

Simons, J. (2002). *Animal Rights and the Politics of Literary Representation*. New York: Palgrave.

Chapter III

Hans Christian Andersen as a Social Observer

Scott Mellor

The question of what is an appropriate topic for literature has been debated for centuries. Even today, the news media, parents, and schools frequently argue about whether books like *The Adventures of Huckleberry Finn*, *To Kill a Mockingbird*, and even *Harry Potter* are suitable for school-age children, due to their treatment of such potentially divisive topics as race relations, political oppression, and religious belief. Although Hans Christian Andersen is regarded as one of the world's most beloved children's authors, his fairy tales are not just pretty stories of wonder and fantasy; many of them also deal with serious social issues that reflect Andersen's critical engagement with both the issues of his time and the artistic movements that influenced his work.

During the 18th and 19th centuries, European authors and scholars argued about whether it was appropriate to bring up social issues in literature. The

Enlightenment, which was a major artistic and philosophical movement during the 18th century, was replete with texts promoting social change. The French author Jean-Jacques Rousseau (1712–1778), for example, argued for the engagement of social ideas through public debate. During the Enlightenment, reason was the order of the day. The world could be observed and described rationally. The united kingdom of Denmark-Norway had one well-known advocate for Enlightenment thinking, Ludvig Holberg (1684–1754). Born in Bergen, Norway, he later moved to Denmark, and as a result, both countries claim him as the father of their modern literature.

By the mid-18th century in the German states, a socially critical literary movement grew as a reaction to the Enlightenment called *Sturm und Drang* (Storm and Stress), which is considered proto-Romantic. Whereas the Enlightenment had stressed rationalism and society, *Sturm und Drang* authors began to consider the extremes of emotion and the subjectivity of the individual as an aesthetic choice. Two German authors, Johann Wolfgang von Goethe (1749–1832) and Friedrich Schiller (1759–1805), who had been very engaged with *Sturm und Drang*, ended their association with the movement. Together with the German philosopher Johann Gottfried Herder (1744–1803), they began a new era called Weimar Classicism, a movement that attempted to fuse *Sturm und Drang*, Classical, and Enlightenment ideas together. Herder's notion of the *Volksseele*, or "spirit of the people," influenced such Romantic scholars as Jacob (1785–1863) and Wilhelm Grimm (1786–1859), the collectors of the German folk tales that would, in turn, influence so greatly the works of Hans Christian Andersen. Of the three—Goethe, Schiller, and Herder—only Goethe would live into the Romantic period proper and become the grand man of Romantic letters.

In his later life, Goethe argued against realism, politics, and social issues as appropriate topics for literature. In his opinion, literature should concern itself with the good, the beautiful, and the true. In a letter to Johann Peter Eckermann (1792–1854), a German author, written in March 1832 (the year of his death), Goethe maintained that political issues and artists' works should not be combined, arguing, "If a poet wants to have a political effect, he must surrender to a party, and as he does this, he is lost as a poet" (*Goethezeitportal* 2013).[1] By the beginning of the 19th century, in the aftermath of the French revolution, many German authors, even those whose works had previously been representative of the Enlightenment style, wanted to see a return to a focus on beauty in art and literature. Danish writers at the beginning of the century drew upon many German influences, and were thus affected by this shift in orientation. This aesthetic view became very popular among Danish Romantic writers and artists, who turned away from politics and realism in order to focus on nature and beauty. Denmark drew heavily on German literature at the beginning of the 19th century, but Danish literature returned to realistic writing and social issues in the 1870s and became tremendously influential in Germany toward the end of the century.

---

1   The translation is my own: "*Sowie ein Dichter politisch wirken will, muß er sich einer Partei hingeben; und sowie er dieses tut, ist er als Poet verloren.*"

Although Hans Christian Andersen is commonly regarded as a Romantic writer, and many of his texts demonstrate Romantic characteristics, Andersen's texts do not always conform to the line of thought that only the good and the beautiful are true and worthy of attention. In his story, "The Shadow," published in 1847, the scholar is seen as foolish for publishing works that view only the good and the beautiful as true; a position which leads to the scholar's demise. The text suggests that he is blind to the ambition of his emancipated shadow, whose actions are dictated by his experience that it is the bad and ugly which are true; a truth the shadow seems to know at the expense of the good and the beautiful.[2] The tale seems to conclude that as complete humans, we must know the good *and* the bad, the beautiful *and* the ugly in order to know the truth, a sentiment also suggested in "The Nightingale," from 1844. At the end of this tale, when the

Figure 3.1 Edmund Dulac's 1911 illustration of "The Nightingale" shows Death crouching on the Chinese emperor's chest.

emperor is on his deathbed, the nightingale, a symbol for the artist, returns to the emperor and demonstrates the life-giving property of art by saving the emperor through its song. The emperor begs the nightingale to stay, but the bird says it cannot stay confined in the palace, suggesting that art must be free to be true art. The bird says it will return to tell the emperor all that goes on in his realm: "I shall sit on the branch outside your window and sing to you. And my song shall make you happy and make you thoughtful. I shall sing not only of those who are happy but also of those who suffer. I shall sing of the good and of the evil that happen around you, and yet are hidden from you" (Andersen 1974, 212). The text ends with a cautionary warning directed at those who find truth in art. The nightingale tells the emperor not to reveal the source of his information, for people will not accept that he gets his truth through art.

Andersen retained his Romantic disposition throughout his literary life, but he also makes observations about the social issues of his day in many of his tales, challenging Goethe's view that the two are incompatible. His use of a storyteller's language and fantastic images like talking ducks and singing mermaids identifies him as a Romantic, despite the fact that he also dealt with social problems. He did not, however, embrace the Modern

---

2   See Karin Sanders' article in this volume for more in-depth discussion of "The Shadow."

Breakthrough, the French-inspired movement toward realism in literature, which became popular in Denmark toward the end of Andersen's life. As the name suggests, the Realists believed that depictions in literature should be an accurate reflection of life, and Modern Breakthrough writers hoped to create awareness of social issues, especially regarding class and gender, through realistic depictions in order to promote social change. Unlike authors of the Modern Breakthrough, Andersen rarely, if ever, tries to actively promote a specific social agenda. Instead, in contrast to the omniscient, authoritative narrators favored by Modern Breakthrough writers, Andersen's distanced, subjective narrators simply make observations about some of the social problems of the time and allow the reader to draw his or her own conclusions. Good examples of such social observation can be found in Andersen's tales, "Grief" and "The Watchman of the Tower."

"Grief" (1853)

Though Andersen is best known for writing fairy stories, often rewriting or even imitating folktale genres in the style of the Brothers Grimm, "Grief" shows his diversity as a writer and his interest in social issues. This compact, enigmatic story, written in 1853, is composed in a more realistic style than many of his better-known texts, such as "The Little Mermaid" or "The Ugly Duckling." It deals with changing social structures that were of concern to Danes at the time, as well as with issues of free enterprise and governance that are still debated today. For Denmark in the second half of the 19th century, this text was reflective of changing social and political conditions. In 1660, King Frederick III had established absolute monarchy in Denmark, which gave the king ultimate authority over the state. By the time of Andersen's birth, this had been the governing norm for almost 150 years. However, in 1848, King Frederick VI presided over a shift from absolute monarchy to a constitutional monarchy and parliamentary system of government. How would Denmark be changed as a result of this new system? Would it be to the people's benefit? Another change that was in the air and would come the year after this tale was published was the dissolution of the guilds. The guilds, in essence trade monopolies, had been largely in control of commerce since the Middle Ages. Now the country was moving toward a different economic model, that of free enterprise. Andersen was acutely aware of the control the guilds had had over people's lives; his own father could not afford to become a guild member and was therefore not allowed to take on apprentices, which would have allowed him some advancement in his own situation. But how would this new economic model work for people? These are a few of the questions that Andersen takes up in "Grief."

According to the narrator, "Grief" is a "story in two parts" (414). Early in the tale, the reader may be lulled into complacency when assured by the narrator that "the first [part of the story] is not really necessary but it provides background and that is always useful" (414). At the end of the tale, however, the narrator lets us know that, if we have not already figured it out, there is more to this story than we may have realized, announcing: "That is the story and if you haven't understood it then you can buy stock in the widow's tannery" (414). Andersen seems to be having some fun with his audience, trying to convince us that the first part is not really necessary, while at the same time wanting us to look past the surface of the tale and see its important social meaning. This line is a challenge, and alerts the reader to the fact that there is more going on in the text than the surface narrative. The astute reader quickly discovers that the background information in the first part of the story has as much to do with the underlying import of the narrative as the second and draws in some of the same social issues.

"Grief" is written in the first person, but the text says nothing directly about the narrator's identity; most of what is known must be inferred. The effect of the first person narration is to give the reader an intimate perspective, a sense of proximity to what is being told. The reader is drawn into the story and can even believe that the narrator may be telling us a true story. The narrator begins by mentioning, "We were visiting friends who lived in a manor house out in the country" (414). The narrator is a friend of the owner of the manor house, who is presumably rather well off. When a woman comes to the manor house to ask for investment money for her tannery, she is told to write a letter of petition using the owner of the manor house's titles: "War Commissary General, Knight of the Danish Flag, etc." (414). We understand from this that the owner is high up in the traditional, feudal hierarchy and male, since women at this time could not hold such titles. We are not told the narrator's gender, but since his friend is probably male, we might assume that he, too, is male.

These kinds of clues can help us begin to understand that the story is dealing with social class issues of the time. We can infer that the narrator belongs to the same social class as his friend, since the gap between the classes was great at this period in Danish history, and they rarely mixed in social settings. The woman in the text appears to be of a different class and gender from the narrator, which may explain her comment to him, while writing out the manor owner's titles on her petition, that "I am only a woman" (414). There is a distance of class and privilege between the woman and the narrator. The encounter in the first half of the story exemplifies the old way, a traditional, patriarchal, feudal society. In the second half of the story, this society is contrasted with the new, modern society, but the changes are hinted at in this first part. The woman is called a widow and, though we are not told, it seems likely that she has inherited her tannery from her husband. Her self-effacing comment about being "only a woman" is undercut by the ambitious nature of what she is trying to accomplish. The text tells us that she is trying to sell stock—in other words, to raise capital—in order to upgrade her tannery. Though she will lose complete control of the shop, she will be able to improve and compete in the new economic reality and survive. This text was written toward the beginning of the industrial revolution in Denmark. This first part of the story, the part that was described as "not really necessary," therefore sets up the observations on social change that emerge from the second part of the story.

In terms of narrative style, Andersen likes to add comedy and whimsy to his stories. He frequently adds small, humorous details to his tales. Though serious topics are being discussed, political and economic systems, the narrative is fun to read. In "Grief," the widow's dog provides some comic relief, though even here the astute reader may see it being

Figure 3.2 Vilhelm Pedersen's 1853 depiction of the widow and her dog in "Grief."

used as commentary. Her dog is taken along on this venture, we are informed, "for his health and amusement, and so he thought he wasn't supposed to be put down on the floor" (414). The widow tells us that the dog is "like a member of the family: faithful but bad tempered; and that's my grandchildren's fault. They like to play 'getting married' and the dog has to be a bridesmaid, and that tires him out, the poor thing!" (414). He is an old, grumpy dog who adds a humorous and humanizing component to the story and who ties the two parts of the story together. We might also venture to see a metaphor in which the dog represents the old feudal system of Denmark, with the aristocracy being carried by the lower classes; a system which is familiar and which is changing, or dying as the dog will die. Despite the narrator's reassurance, "That was the first part of the story, the one that could have been skipped" (414), the astute reader knows that it was actually of vital importance.

The second half of the story begins with the narrator's announcement: "The lap dog died; that is the second part" (415). Though death and existential crisis are frequently addressed in Andersen's writings, the reader quickly discovers that is not the focus in this story, despite its title. The narrator is in town and finds himself on an upper story of a building overlooking the widow's tannery. The widow's grandchildren are making a grave for the old lap dog. The death of the dog, however, is not the cause of the titular grief. There is no reference in the narrative to anyone's, even the widow's, grief over the death of the dog. Instead, we must look elsewhere for the source of grief.

Like their grandmother, the children conducting the funeral prove themselves to be entrepreneurial. They wish to sell tickets to the dog's grave:

> The oldest of the boys, an enterprising young lad of seven, suggested that they should exhibit the grave to anyone in the street who would care to see it. The entrance fee should be one button, for that was something that every boy who wore suspenders owned; and he could even pay for a girl without losing his trousers. The proposal was carried unanimously. (415)

In this passage, the narrator introduces the idea of free enterprise; the boy is able to make money by merely having an idea and exploiting it. In the style of Denmark's newly democratic political system, they take a vote and the proposal carries. In the old system, there was a tremendous gap between rich and poor, and new ideas could be held back by the traditional structures enforced by the guilds. This new system will allow for ideas to be vetted and implemented, if a consensus can be reached. The tale seems to offer a positive endorsement of this innovation. However, there is criticism here too, for they are selling death, and their democratic system fails to allow everyone to participate. At the end of the tale, the narrator tells of a young girl who does not have a button and thus cannot get in to see the dog: "She didn't utter a word nor did she cry; but every time the gate was opened she peeked in. She didn't own a button and therefore she stood dejected outside the gate all afternoon, until the last children had left" (415). Under the old system, those on the outside were not able to participate politically or economically to their full advantage, but the text suggests that the new system will be the same. The girl is still on the outside, looking in.

"Grief" concludes with a statement from the narrator, "Now that was grief, a sorrow as sharp as a grownup's can be! We saw it from above; and the little girl's sorrow—like many of our own—was laughable when seen from above" (415). The narrator acknowledges the grief of the little girl, but also suggests that it is ridiculous, to outside observers, at least, though not to the girl herself. The first part of the story establishes the social distance between the narrator and the woman. In the second, the story employs another type of distance, namely physical distance. The narrator observes the events from above. Like a god in his heaven or a king on his throne, the physical distance is supposed to allow for the narrator's objectivity; his actual distance from the events affords him objective clarity. The girl is sad, but over what? Not seeing the dead dog's grave. In the end, is this really something to be grieved over? And yet, the text subtly undermines the authority of the narrator to make such a judgment. Given the social distance between him and the people he watches, how can he fully appreciate the life that he is observing? He lacks the social context for the young girl's grief. The social distance undermines the objectivity the physical distance is trying to create. The strategy of exploring the subjective over the objective is a Romantic one, which Andersen repurposes in order to comment on social issues.

"The Watchman of the Tower" (1859)

While the topics discussed in "Grief" are of questionable appropriateness to the Romantic sensibility although the narrative strategies conform to that paradigm, both the subject matter and the narrative style of "The Watchman of the Tower" (1859) diverge from Romantic norms. There is no real plot to this story, which sometimes confuses students assigned to read it, and there is little description of nature, emotion, or beauty in any form. Andersen's oeuvre as a mature author began in 1835 with a volume called *Tales Told for Children*, in which he retells and imitates folk tales, which were beloved by Romantics for their perceived authenticity. This simple beginning lends itself to the idea persistent even today that he is a writer for children. In this text, that perception is inverted. This is not a tale told for children, but rather a complex story about knowledge, doubt, and religion.

"The Watchman of the Tower" is a framed narrative, a story with two other stories embedded within it, which can make it difficult for readers to know where to concentrate their attention. The focus of the frame story is the narrator telling the audience of two occasions on which he had visited his friend, Ole, who is the watchman of the tower. In the story Andersen points to social and philosophical change in the past and their effects, illuminating changes taking place in the present and their possible outcomes, which are yet unknown. One example of this is the tower itself. The tower in question is the Round Tower in Copenhagen, which is still a prominent feature of the city skyline today and which plays two roles in this text. Christian IV (1577-1648) had the tower built for Tycho Brahe (1564-1601), the prominent Danish astronomer. Brahe's observations were used to prove that the Earth was not the center of the universe, an idea first proposed by the Polish astronomer Nicolaus Copernicus (1473-1543). The placement of the Earth in the cosmos held considerable religious significance that was challenged during the 16th and 17th centuries and was a controversial scientific topic in its day. The astute reader will juxtapose the changes that occurred in the two eras, along with the social and religious strife and wonder. The text only indirectly refers to new theories of the creation of the earth and evolution of humans, but it links the controversies by using the Round Tower of Copenhagen: in the case of the former, the Earth not being at the center of the universe, an argument that had been largely accepted by Andersen's day; and in the latter, the new theories on the age of the Earth and of evolution, an argument that still causes controversy in our day. The text engages in a discussion of the role of religion and science in our lives, a discussion that is still relevant for us today.

The second role the Round Tower plays is that it was the tallest building in Copenhagen in Andersen's day. In addition to the use of first-person narration, which creates a subjective point of view in the text that is often unreliable, another narrative feature that links the text "Grief" with "The Watchman of the Tower" is that both use physical distance in the tale to create a sense of narrative objectivity toward the human condition, and then undermines that supposed objectivity. The narrators are removed from the emotional state of the people being observed, and feel they are able to draw objective conclusions. The narrator in "Grief," through his physical distance, sees the girl's grief over not having seen the dog's grave as laughable, but his social distance may have compromised his objectivity gained by physical distance. In "The Watchman of the Tower," the watchman, Ole, does not participate in life, but simply watches people from above, maintaining a physical distance between observed and observer. He calls people ants; although they see themselves as distinctive at ground level, he sees them as all the same from above. The tower affords him that perspective through that physical distance. At the same time, however, his physical distance may give him objectivity, but his lack of participation in real life calls the validity of his conclusions into question.

The narrator describes Ole as "an amusing, talkative fellow, who seemed to poke fun at most things and yet was serious at heart" (Andersen, 615), but he leaves it to the reader to decide what kind of a person Ole is and whether the observations he makes about the human condition may be flawed. Ole prides himself on his elevated position in the world— "Everything in the world goes up and down and I can't get any farther up than I am right now," he exclaims (615)—but his concerns are sometimes trivial. Ole once held a position as assistant teacher for a deacon, but he lost the job due to a disagreement with his employer over English blacking. Ole's contract included room, board, laundry, and boot polish. English blacking was an expensive way to shine shoes, and Ole felt he deserved the more expensive polish, but when the deacon would only pay for lard, Ole accused him of "miserliness and vanity," which led to his dismissal. The narrator reports that Ole holds tight to his sense of having been wronged: "What Ole had demanded from the deacon, he also demanded from the world: English blacking, and all he ever got was lard!" (615). Ole holds a high opinion of himself that the reader may question, but even he, "someone as loftily placed as I am" (615), occasionally regards himself as a zero when confronted with new knowledge about the world.

We are not told how the narrator and Ole first met, only that they have a habit of meeting once a year, just after New Year's, and that this tale will concern two such visits. On the narrator's first visit, Ole compares two worldviews, the scientific and the religious. The 19th century was a time of changing understanding of our world throughout Europe and America. *On the Origin of the Species*, by Charles Darwin (1809–1882), was published in 1859, the same year as Andersen's "The Watchman of the Tower." It is doubtful Andersen had direct knowledge of the work, as he could not read English, but the ideas Darwin put forth were already being hinted at by earlier works and by other scientists. Despite his upbringing in Christian Denmark, Ole prioritizes scientific over religious thought, which would have been a very controversial stance at this time. The narrator tells us, "Among the books which I had lately lent Ole, was one which had greatly rejoiced and occupied him. It was a geological book, containing an account of the cobblestones" (615). The books represent the relatively new understanding of our world through scientific discovery. Scientific learning was changing the way people saw the world. Ole tries to put the new knowledge in the language of the old when he says:

> Yes, they certainly are old Methuselahs, those cobblestones! ... Thank you for lending me the book, it has made me discard many old notions and has given me a different outlook upon the world. I am eager to read more books of that kind. The greatest of all romances is the story of our earth. Too bad that the first volumes are written in a language we have not yet learned. Only after one has read the stones, the layers of earth as they were formed through periods of climatic changes, do the living characters in the romance step forth. Mr. Adam and Mrs. Eve do not appear before the sixth volume. Many readers will find that a little too late, but I don't care. ... It is the history of millions of years of constant advancement. (Andersen, 615–16)

Thanks to the narrator's scientific books, Ole has come to understand that the world is not thousands of years old, as was taught by church doctrine, but much older than Adam and Eve. His newfound enlightenment gives him a new perspective on human society. He notes, "It is amusing to think that everyone, even those who have their boots polished with English blacking, are merely ants with a minute of life in their little bodies. True, there are ranks in the anthill, and some wear ribbons and have titles, but ants they are. One feels oneself so small and unimportant compared to these cobblestones, with their millions of years of history behind them" (615).

With his newfound scientific understanding of the world, Ole feels superior to the people he observes. When he describes how the educated elite of Copenhagen flock to the island of Amager, not far outside the old walls of the city, during the celebration of the New Year,

Ole compares his countrymen's festivities to the alleged flight of witches to Brocken for their annual pagan celebration:

> But you do know about the witches and how they fly to the mountain in Germany called Brocken, on Midsummer night, and there keep a witches' Sabbath. Well, we have a local affair that is something like it. I call it "the wild crowd rushing to Amager." It takes place New Year's Eve and all the bad poets and poetesses, journalists, and artists of notoriety and no talent participate. They fly through the air on their pens and brushes out to Amager. It is not so far away, only ten miles or so. They would never have made it to Brocken; a journalist's pen is no witch's broom. I watch them every New Year's Eve, and I could mention most of them by name but I won't, they are dangerous people to cross. (616)

By using the story of the witches flying to the mountain, Ole demonstrates both his knowledge of and disdain for folk belief, and may be equating religion with such folk belief. His comparison of witches with a crowd of "bad poets and poetesses, journalists, and artists of notoriety and no talent" makes the witches' flight to Brocken commonplace rather than supernatural. Ole is contemptuous of such mediocre artists and thinkers, but he is also wary of them.

Toward the end of the first visit, the conversation again turns to the contrast between science and folk belief. The narrator and Ole see four shooting stars light up the sky. Ole remarks that science does not yet know what a shooting star is, though it is understood that it will be explained someday. In folk belief, a shooting star is an omen, often seen as a harbinger of death. Ole has his own fanciful, artistic idea; a shooting star is the thanks for those who have done good on earth. He combines his own views with traditional folk belief when he maintains that the shooting star falls on the benefactor's grave. Ole suggests a specific grave when he states, "I am sure it landed in Sorø: a bouquet for Holberg's coffin, a thanks from the many who have enjoyed his wonderful comedies" (618). Ole makes another link with the philosophical controversies of the past by evoking the Enlightenment writer, Ludvig Holberg. Though Andersen may or may not have had it in mind, Holberg's play *Erasmus Montanus* (1723) deals with the social implications of new learning on Danish society. Ole acknowledges gratitude to Holberg for his plays and contribution to society, but ends on a self-deprecating note, stating that no shooting star will fall on his grave; "I will never receive English blacking. ...

Figure 3.3 This 1923 illustration of "The Watchman of the Tower" by L. Rhead depicts the "wild crowd rushing to Amager" on New Year's Eve.

Lard is my fate" (618). Ole feels his contributions will not be appreciated, but the reader may question whether he has made any at all.

By contrast, the second visit demonstrates the humorous and humanizing whimsy that Andersen often employs in his texts, as well as offering useful advice about the risks of excessive drinking. After witnessing the overindulgences of yet another New Year's Eve, Ole offers this wisdom: In the first two glasses are found health and a beautiful life. In the third is Cupid and love, but at the fourth, stop—for the fifth will only cause sentimental weeping. "In the sixth glass sits the Devil himself; he is a little well-dressed man, most charming and pleasant" (619). In Scandinavian folkloric tradition, the devil was often a well-dressed man, and Andersen draws on this. The text tells us that the devil will lead you to his house, not yours, and recounts the "old legend about a saint who was ordered to experience one of the seven deadly sins. He decided that drunkenness was the least of them. But as soon as he got drunk, then he committed the other six sins." The early Christian Church used these seven deadly sins to educate the people of mankind's tendency to sin; they included Gluttony, Sloth, Avarice (Greed), Pride, Lust, Envy, and Wrath. They are paired by the early Church with Seven Virtues: Faith, Hope, Charity, Fortitude, Justice, Prudence, and Temperance.

Although Andersen does not mention the seven virtues, they are implicitly invoked by Ole's mention of the seven deadly sins, which brings the narrative back to the question of how truth is to be found, whether through science or religion or superstition. Just as the tale has blended references to folklore, religious belief, and scientific discoveries, Ole concludes by suggesting that truth may be found in a variety of ways. With regard to his own story, he says, "It can be told both with English blacking and with lard. I have used both." Although Ole once felt strongly enough about insisting on blacking to cost him his job, he has learned by observation of the people around him that lard can get the job done just as well. In the end, the reader may conclude that perhaps science, religion, and folklore can all be used to explain the human condition.

Works Cited

Andersen, H. C. (1974). *The Complete Fairy Tales and Stories*, translated by Erik Christian Haugaard. New York: Doubleday.

Borchmeyer, Dieter. "Goethes Allianz mit Schiller" *Goethezeitportal*. http://www.goethezeitportal.de/wissen/dichtung/schnellkurs-goethe/goethes-allianz-mit-schiller.html

Further Readings

Bredsdorff, Elias (1975). *Hans Christian Andersen: The Story of his Life and Work 1805–1875*. New York: Scribner.

Lockhart, Paul Douglas (2007). *Denmark, 1513–1660: The Rise and Decline of a Renaissance Monarchy*. Oxford, UK: UP.

Ogilvie, Sheilagh (2011). *Institutions and European Trade: Merchant Guilds, 1000–1800*. Cambridge, UK: UP.

Rossel, Sven H., ed. (1992). *A History of Danish Literature*. University of Nebraska Press.

Chapter IV

The Visionary Trickster

The Role of the Artist in Hans Christian Andersen's Fairy Tales

Jakob Holm

What is more important—a work of art or the artist who created it? Without the artist, there would be no work of art, but without the work of art, the artist would be nothing. The term "artist" encompasses not just visual artists and performers, but also writers and poets, all of whom stand in a competitive relationship to their own works, but writers perhaps most of all, since their stories take on lives of their own after being told. Hans Christian Andersen, who was a gifted performer and visual artist as well as a famous writer, struggled with this conundrum throughout his life, as he created his own literary masterpieces and sent them out into the world. Many of his tales are world-famous today, from "The Ugly Duckling" to "The Emperor's New Clothes," but many people know nothing about the man who created them, not even that he wrote the tales they love. Film versions of some of his tales, such as Disney's *The Little Mermaid*, have become so internationally famous in their own right that Andersen's original tale has been all but forgotten. Andersen himself can be blamed for this state of affairs, since his tales are so memorable and universal, his characters so vividly drawn, that they exist independently of their creator. Kjeld Hedtoft argues that Andersen's "visually artistic approach, converted into literature, is the essential reason for the ease with which his writings have succeeded, despite often inadequate translations, in crossing national borders. People may not have fully appreciated the stylistic or philosophical subtlety, but the actual *picture* sank in" (1977, 8).

To understand how Andersen himself felt about being in competition with his own creations for fame and immortality, all we need do is look at his fairy tales, for Andersen often wrote stories about art and the role of the artist, sometimes metaphorically and sometimes very directly. For example, one of Andersen's last fairy tales, "The Professor and the Flea" (1872), is one of many examples of how Andersen addresses the psychological and creational aspects of the production of art in an allegorical way. This story tells of a self-proclaimed "professor" who travels the world with a performing flea, but feels neglected when his audience prefers the flea to him. By depicting the tension between the huckster and his talented flea, Andersen explores the relationship between the artist, his art, and his audience, as well as commenting on the dangers artists face as a result of success.[1] In this chapter, we'll compare Andersen's treatment of art and the role of the artist in three tales—"The Flying Trunk," "The Pen and the Inkwell," and "The Collar"—that illustrate, from different angles, the challenges that artists face. Despite artists' longing for connectedness with and admiration from their audiences, Andersen cautions that the storyteller must resist the temptation to believe in his own tales and his own genius too completely or risk losing everything, including his self-respect.

The Romantic Cult of the Artist

It is not surprising that Andersen thought a great deal about the status of art and the role of the artist, since Romanticism, the dominant aesthetic movement in Europe at the beginning of Andersen's career, was obsessed with art. The Romantics longed for a feeling of connectedness with the universal, and they believed you could achieve that through art. Naturally, this focus on art gave the artist an important role, because he or she was suddenly seen not just as a mere craftsman, but as a visionary and mediator, a person able to connect other people with the hidden truths in life. Furthermore, the Romantics celebrated the cult of the individual and the genius, both of which can be embodied in the figure of the artist. The cult surrounding the composers Beethoven and Wagner, who were worshipped almost like gods by their fans during the 19th century, is an example of that phenomenon.

---

1   See Nate Kramer's chapter in this volume for a more in-depth discussion of "The Professor and the Flea."

However, this kind of deification could have grave consequences for artists, because it turns out that it can be immensely difficult for them to feel special and unique without losing touch with ordinary people and their concerns. If an artist is regarded as a craftsman, he's a part of everyday life, exactly as if he were a shoemaker or a goldsmith; but as a visionary, the artist is often put on a pedestal and set apart from ordinary people, which can make him or her become disconnected from real life. This dilemma caused many artists of the time to have trouble dealing with basic human relationships and responsibilities. In Andersen's case, this was true both when he was too poor to be able to afford more than a blanket on the floor of a brothel to sleep on and when he was so famous that wealthy people across Europe begged him to come visit them. In fact, Hans Christian Andersen moved around so much that he didn't even own a bed of his own until he was 61 years old, let alone a house. He never married or had children, but he still became one of the most beloved storytellers for generations of children around the world.

The expectation that the artist should be able to dig deeper and see farther than the common man made Andersen and many of his contemporaries self-conscious about the production of art and about their role as artists. Even though the idea of being set apart and special was delightful for a person as vain as Andersen, it was also a burden, because it invariably led to penetrating self-examination: What can you do if you want to immerse yourself in life, be praised, travel, and fall in love, but your artistic sensibility and extreme focus on yourself keep you isolated? How can you remain as connected to life as you need to be in order to know and write about it and yet aloof enough at the same time to have artistic credibility? How can you manage this double movement? What if your talent falls short of genius? Is art authentic even if it is the product of trickery? What price must the artist pay for his genius? These questions, although not necessarily posed explicitly, underlie many of Andersen's tales.

Andersen was by no means the only person to ponder these matters in his own time or since. Individual artists have struggled with such questions since the beginning of the Romantic era. Artists who internalize the Romantic notion of the role of artist as visionary, which persists to this day, discover that it can undermine their confidence in their own work: they have to deal with both their own self-doubt and the conviction that they are, in fact, capable of grasping some deeper truth to share with the world. The psychological hardship of such pressure has driven many writers to substance abuse, including Ernest Hemingway, Truman Capote, Jack Kerouac, F. Scott Fitzgerald, William Faulkner, and Raymond Chandler, to name just a few well-known 20th-century American literary drunkards.

Like these more recent authors, Andersen struggled with crippling insecurity. Instead of trying to solve it with alcohol or other kinds of abuse, Andersen quieted his fears with a steady diet of admiration. That was the psychologically crippling drug that he needed in large doses, and which he received especially from members of the Danish and German upper classes, whose members he visited on a regular basis and whose riches and honorary titles he admired in return. Although he had a difficult time with romantic relationships and suffered from unrequited love for a string of women and men, Andersen's sensitivity to the inner life of children, his infatuation with the notion of being in love, and his moralizing tales were appreciated in the bourgeois salons and nurseries, earning him the regard of powerful patrons who helped him in his quest for fame and fortune. However, admiration was not enough to soothe Andersen's insecurities completely, which is fortunate for his readers, because it drove him to address his daunting task as a storyteller, his fears and his longings, in many of his tales, including not only "The Pen and the Inkwell," "The Flying Trunk," and "The Collar," which we will discuss below, but also such seminal tales as "Psyche," "Auntie Toothache," "The Shadow," and "The Nightingale."

Andersen's way of coping with his existential worries, combined with his storytelling skills, enabled him to explore the complexity of the artist's role and his conflicted relationship to his own art. This practice of addressing the actual production of art, often called meta-fiction, is a common narrative strategy in modern literature, particularly among postmodern authors like Italo Calvino and Paul Auster. More than a century before it became popular, however, Andersen frequently reflected on the nature of storytelling in the middle of the stories he was telling. This trait in Andersen's narrative style is already present in one of his first stories, *The Princess on the Pea*,[2] which ends with the words "Now that was a real story!" (Andersen 2004, 30). The final line is added as a reminder to the reader that the story was just a story, acting as an ironic commentary on the utterance situation and the artificiality of storytelling. It reconnects the reader with his or her own reality (it was "just" a story), and it reconnects the narrator with his reality: Now, I've told you a story, and I'm out of here (i.e., out of the fictional universe I just created).

Andersen's oeuvre is full of examples of tales in which he explores the relationship between the artist and the production of art from many different angles. In some, like "The Emperor's New Clothes," he depicts artists who are charlatans, while in others, like "The Nightingale," he praises the healing, redemptive power of art. The stories we'll be examining in this chapter all show in exemplary fashion how artists struggle with the temptation to believe their own stories and admire their own greatness. The storyteller may lie and cheat in the process of creating art, but if his lying and cheating begin to interfere with real life, he will end up paying a price for it.

"The Flying Trunk" (1838)

Let's begin by considering how the conflict between the artist and his art plays out in "The Flying Trunk." The story deals with a merchant's son, who wastes his fortune and has to make his way in the world by his wits as a storyteller. Wearing a dressing gown and slippers, he flies in an enchanted trunk to the land of the Turks, where he claims to be a god and woos the princess with fanciful stories. He wins her hand but loses his trunk to a stray firework spark, thus condemning himself to wander the world telling stories forever. It's a story that

---

2   The title of this story is frequently translated as "The Princess and the Pea," but the original Danish preposition dealing with the princess's relationship to the pea is "on," which is how Tiina Nunally chooses to translate it.

displays a lot of Andersen's usual narrative tricks such as irony, humiliation of the proud, transformation of life situations, and mystical, but treacherous helpers—i.e., the trunk—but it also deals extensively with the artist's role as a trickster pretending to be a visionary, as well as the difficulty of pursuing personal relationships when your life and your livelihood are based on deception.

A central part of the tale is a story within a story that the merchant's son tells to the king and the queen, which exemplifies how Andersen sees the relation between the storyteller, his tale, and his audience. While the frame story is set in an exotic palace and the stakes of success are social advancement and marital bliss, the story within the story takes place in a kitchen among anthropomorphized kitchenware and is a scathing parody of bourgeois Danish society, with all its conflicts and hunger for news. The turmoil in the kitchen mirrors the political unrest in Denmark at the time, and shows how narrow-minded people end up being if they never get out of their own environment. In addition, the story suggests that the more specialized society gets, the more distance there will be between people, as is the case in the kitchen in the story, where all the different tools have a highly specialized skill set, but can't relate to each other when it comes to mutual communication and understanding.

How does this societal movement toward specialization affect the artist or storyteller? This story seems to warn that it could reduce the artist to a mere entertainer. This position is exemplified by the earthenware pot, who suggests: "'Let's have an evening of entertainment. I'll start. I'm going to tell you about something that everyone has experienced. You don't have to think too hard about it, and that's quite pleasant.'" (Andersen 2004, 127). The

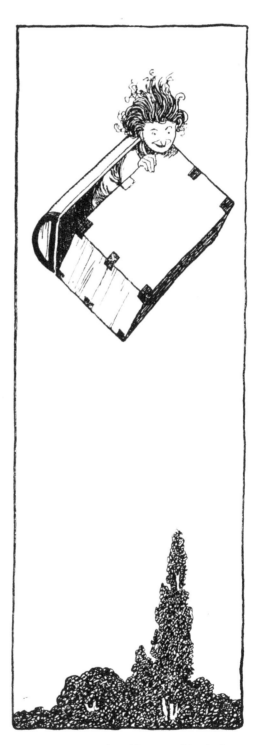

Figure 4.1 W. Heath Robinson's whimsical 1913 illustration of "The Flying Trunk."

Figure 4.2 Hans Tegner's illustration, "The King, the Queen, and the whole court taking tea with the merchant's son" (1900), captures the artist's ability to enrapture his audience.

narrator's dry tone reveals that Andersen doesn't think very highly about this kind of mindless entertainment, as he doesn't see fit to use any creative energy to tell what this story is about, except that it follows the basic rules about storytelling and has a beginning, middle, and end. Furthermore, the earthenware pot's tale is representative of the Biedermeier style of literature, which focuses on the domestic sphere rather than on nature or the imagination: "I spent my youth with a quiet family. The furniture was polished, the floors washed, and the clean curtains were put up every two weeks" (128). The other kitchen implements crown the pot with a parsley garland in appreciation of its story, reflecting the popularity of Biedermeier style in the mid-19th century, but Andersen shows that the pot's story doesn't change the dynamics in the kitchen—it is pure diversion, a minuscule distraction from the general mayhem. In this tale within a tale, Andersen frets that the artist must resign himself to a role as a pure entertainer, no longer be the discloser of the hidden things in life, because the audience will be tone-deaf—just as the kitchenware takes an instant liking to the earthenware pot's story because it

is recognizable: There is an immediate identification between the story and their own surroundings. It is pure surface, and nothing else.

Taken as a whole, however, "The Flying Trunk" asserts a much more complex role for the artist in the way it sets up the relationship between the sender, message, and receiver/audience. The tale functions on three levels of that communication: on the level of the narrated tale, Hans Christian Andersen is the sender, the message is the tale, "The Flying Trunk," directed at the actual reader. We find the same structure replicated within the tale itself, but now the merchant's son is the sender, the allegorical story about the kitchenware is the message, and the king and queen are the audience. Finally, in the tale within the tale, the story the earthenware pot tells the kitchenware reproduces the communicative situation once more. In all three cases, Andersen's project is to convey to the reader that you have to look beyond the face value of a story when you approach it: Just as the kitchen implements shouldn't have been so enthusiastic about the pot's banal tale, the princess and her parents shouldn't have been deceived by the merchant's son's clever storytelling, and Andersen's own readers should look carefully for the true meaning of the story about the merchant's son's rise and fall. If you don't look behind the immediate surface of a story, Andersen seems to suggest, you will be deceived, and you may—which is worse—confuse art with reality.

That's exactly what happens in the frame story: Art is mistaken for reality. The princess and her parents believe the merchant's son's stories about himself to be true, and they are punished by his failure to appear for the wedding. More serious, however, is the fate of the storyteller himself. In pretending to be more than he is, he loses his sense of reality. His excessive and blind self-assessment is implicit in the narrator's statement after the merchant's son sets off a load of fireworks on the eve of his wedding. The people in the streets cheered and the narrator comments, "Now they understood that it was the Turkish god himself who was to marry the princess" (129). On one level, this remark can be read as a straightforward assessment of the Turks' gullibility for believing the protagonist's deception, but when the reader learns that, immediately after the fireworks display, the merchant's son goes into town to bask in the people's admiration, it becomes clear that he believes in his own divinity. His self-evaluation is pure hubris, revealing that he had stepped over the crucial, invisible line an artist may never cross—namely, the one between reality and art. The punishment of this sweet-talking Don Juan for his hubris is immediate and ironic: As punishment for seducing himself into believing his own stories, a spark—a symbol of artistic inspiration—from the fireworks set fire to the trunk and he loses the very thing that gave him the physical and social mobility to court the princess, so that he must wander about telling stories to earn his keep. From now on, the narrator reports, his fairy tales are "no longer as merry as the one he told about the sulfur matches" (130), which, given that the tale about the kitchen was anything but lighthearted, but on the contrary, rather cynical, is also ironic. However, the merchant's son has learned his lesson and that gives his tales a more serious tone: From now on he will no longer mix up storytelling and reality and no longer try to seduce people, including himself, through his art.

The problem with this tidy resolution is, of course, that people love to be deceived, and deception is fundamental to art. That is another part of Andersen's message: On one hand, art is an illusion, and you have to believe for a while—you have to dive into the plot, suspend your disbelief, accept the fantastic—in order to be moved by its truth and hidden meanings; but on the other hand, although art is entertainment and pleasure, if you don't look critically to see what's behind the surface, if you believe in it for too long, you may end up being tricked. Hence, the artist is a visionary who can convey truth about the big questions of life, but he or she can also be an impostor or seducer.

The conclusion must be that however much a storyteller may desire to belong to the real world, to settle down and marry the princess, he must remember that art comes at the price of isolation. In this statement, some may see a biographical echo: It is well known that Andersen kept the world at arm's length, despite his longing for love and acceptance. He was a detached outsider who knew what would happen if he connected too much with the real world: The elevated status he had earned by virtue of his creative imagination might disappear, never to be regained. Like the merchant's son in his own tale, Hans Christian Andersen was condemned by his own storytelling gift to wander the world telling fairy tales.

"The Pen and the Inkwell" (1860)

While the early tale "The Flying Trunk" warns of the artist's burden, one of Andersen's much later stories, "The Pen and the Inkwell," declares that it is not the artist at all, but the art itself that matters; the artist is just a tool in the hand of God. Once again, Andersen uses an analogy to explore the artist's relationship to his or her own creative power: A pen and an inkwell argue over who deserves more credit for the work of the author who owns and uses them to write his tales. The inkwell claims to be "someone quite extraordinary. From me springs all poetry" (Andersen 1983, 639), but the pen disagrees: "You exist so that I can express upon paper the thoughts that are within me, so that I can write them down. It is the pen that writes!" (639). The premise of the story is ironic, as the reader knows that neither of them deserves the credit for the author's work. Both the pen and the inkwell are just tools, instruments that allow the writer to commit his own genius to paper.

Yet their conversation parallels the author's concurrent experience at a concert featuring a great violinist, where he feels as if "the violin sang by itself and the bow moved by itself; the two were one. One almost forgot their master: the musician who played upon them and gave to these two dead objects a soul. But the poet had not forgotten him; he pondered over it and wrote down his thoughts" (640). The poet's musings reveal the argument between the pen and the inkwell to be an allegory for the role of the artist more generally, in particular man's pride and vanity: The poet realizes that while it is absurd that the violin—or, by analogy, the pen and inkwell—should take credit for the art that is produced through them, it is just as absurd for an artist to claim credit for the works he produces, because he is himself a tool, an instrument upon which God plays: "To Him belongs all honor. We have nothing to pride ourselves upon! Later the poet wrote a parable and called it 'The Genius and His Instrument'" (640). The poet's epiphany doesn't resolve the argument between the pen and the inkwell, both of whom go to sleep believing they have had the last word, but the poet stays awake, full of inspiration: "He felt the cry of his own heart and the spark of the Eternal Master. To Him alone belongs the honor and the glory!" (641).

This tale serves as a gentle reminder to Andersen himself and his fellow artists not to become too proud because of their ability to create art. As Andersen knew well from his personal interactions with many of the leading authors of 19th-century Europe, from Ludwig Tieck to Charles Dickens, many authors—thanks in part to the Romantic cult of the genius that viewed the artist as the discloser of the hidden truths—suffered from a superiority complex. By contrast, Andersen's tale asserts that men are mistaken if they think their creativity and public acclaim are due to their own genius. Of course, human beings control their instruments, whether pen and inkwell or violin and bow, but it is God who creates the spark—the connection between the artist's heart and his ability to express himself.

As in the previous instance, Andersen uses this story as a vehicle for considering the role of the artist in relation to his or her work. Although the style and mood of the two tales are quite different, both tales warn that an artist must not succumb to the temptation to believe too much in his own genius, like the merchant's son in "The Flying Trunk." Instead of calling himself a god, he must always remember that his gift comes from God. Andersen knew from personal experience not only how intoxicating it can be for an artist to be deluged with flattery and admiration, but also how dangerous it would be to believe too much in his own importance. The tale's affirmation of the centrality of divine inspiration at once confirms the Romantic trope of the artist as visionary, and challenges the inevitable sense of self-importance that results from being selected to receive such visions of beauty. The artist must learn to strike the proper balance between pride and humility, to accept that his own greatness is due to the art that he is inspired to produce, if he is to avoid looking as foolish as the pen and the inkwell.

"The Collar" (1848)

Although the final tale that we will examine, the utterly ironic tale, "The Collar," may seem at first glance to have little to do with the production of art or the artist's own role, it is, in fact, yet another allegory about storytelling. The tale focuses on a linen shirt collar, anthropomorphized as a proud, vain fellow full of lies, who, in a desperate attempt to get married, boasts about his own importance to a series of feminine objects, including a garter, an iron, a pair of scissors, and a comb. Later, the collar is sent to the paper factory along with the other rags, where he boasts about his conquests, claiming that the garter drowned herself for his sake, the iron turned black with despair, and the comb lost all her teeth. Remarking on his regret over the garter's death, the collar remarks prophetically, "I have a lot on my conscience. It's about time I was turned into white paper" (Andersen 2004, 263), which is exactly what happens. Of course, he is not redeemed by being made into the very sheet of paper upon which his boastful lies are proclaimed to the world, but is instead exposed to even more ridicule. That is the ultimate situational irony: The collar ends up becoming the physical evidence of his own stupidity and arrogance, as the tale is printed on the paper made from him and the other rags.

So what does this tale teach us about storytelling? The story of the collar reminds us, on one hand, that fictional texts are, by definition, a pack of lies, but on the other hand, fiction can also serve to reveal truths. In this fictional tale about the collar's lies, Andersen presents us with the truth about the collar, about the consequences of telling stories for our own aggrandizement: We will eventually be exposed and become a laughingstock. The same is true for writers: They must be wary of boastfulness and careful not to confuse fiction with reality

The Shirt Collar in its glory.

Figure 4.3 This 1882 engraving by the Dalziel brothers is called "The Shirt Collar in Its Glory."

like the collar does. The collar's motivation is to find a bride, to form a permanent attachment to someone else, but his penchant for telling stories foils his every effort to do so. Andersen seems to be offering yet another warning about the dangers of artists taking themselves too seriously: if the storyteller can't—or won't—differentiate between life and art, because his longing for connectedness is too strong, he is doomed to be ridiculed. Even if the lies he tells are entertaining and sell well, he himself will suffer for boasting about them. At the end of the tale, Andersen's narrator warns, "That's something we should remember, so we don't behave the same way, because we can never tell whether we too might one day end up in the rag bin and be turned into white paper and have our whole story printed on it, even our innermost secrets, and then have to run around talking about them, just like the collar" (263). This is a warning that storytelling can make or break your reputation, because it is the way in which your actions are narrated and interpreted that counts—if nothing is told about you, neither the good nor the bad you have done will be exposed to the world.

As is so often the case with Andersen, this tale has an autobiographical dimension. Throughout his life, Andersen was preoccupied with shaping his own personal history, crafting a fairy tale about his rise to international fame and fortune from the gutters of Odense. In his determination to make his own life a work of art, Andersen published three autobiographies, by means of which he tried to control the narrative of his own life, for example, by romanticizing his childhood poverty and omitting any references to his sister, who worked as a prostitute in Copenhagen. Comparisons between Andersen's letters and published autobiographies reveal that the latter are full of embellishments and half-truths designed to make people think well of him. Andersen understood what was at stake in terms of differentiating between reality and fiction, because he struggled with it himself. He knew that blurring the boundaries between reality and fiction may be an effective strategy for selling books, but can have dire consequences for individuals. Like the collar who longed for a wife or the merchant's son who longed for social ascent, the artist cannot let his longing for connectedness and acceptance dictate his real-life actions: Storytellers may be allowed to cheat and lie in their tales, but they must not fail to distinguish between fact and fantasy, or it will eventually destroy them.

Conclusion

The question of the role of the artist preoccupied Hans Christian Andersen for decades and found expression in dozens of his fairy tales, not just the few we have looked at here. Despite the adulation heaped on him by his countless admirers and fans, Andersen was a lonely man who became increasingly worried toward the end of his life that he would be forgotten, that only his works would remain. Many of his late stories, such as "Psyche" (1861), "The Bronze Pig" (1862), and "Auntie Toothache" (1872), depict the permanence of art in contrast to the transitory nature of human existence and inevitable mortality.

Yet, even as he struggled with the physical pain of his bodily decline and the emotional pain caused by his fear of death, Andersen wrote a story titled, "The Most Incredible Thing" (1870), in which he affirms the interconnectedness of the artist and his or her creations. This tale tells the story of a king who has pledged his daughter's hand in marriage and half of his kingdom as a reward to the person who could do the most incredible thing. The obvious winner is an enormous clock, with moving, speaking figures that announce each new hour, that has been built by "a young man, tenderhearted, childishly happy, a loyal friend, and helpful to his impoverished parents. He deserved the princess and half the kingdom" (Andersen 2004, 406). Before he receives his prize, however, another man walks in with an ax and smashes the clock to bits. In shock, the judges decree that such an unexpected, unwarranted act of wanton destruction is the most unbelievable thing they have witnessed, and name the perpetrator as the winner. At this point in the story, it seems that Andersen may be suggesting either that the creation of art is futile, since it is so much easier to destroy art than to create it, or that the forcefulness of the artist's personality determines his greatness.

The rest of the story, however, offers quite a different message about the respective value of art and the artist. Just as the bride and groom stand at the altar to be married, the resurrected clock marches down the aisle, and the narrator cautions, "Dead people can't rise again—that's something we know for sure—but a work of art can. The body had been shattered, but not the spirit" (407). On one hand, this scene would seem to confirm that art is more important than its creator because of its enduring spirit. The broken figures emerge from the clock and describe the damage that has been done to them, but the bridegroom feels no shame until the last figure, the night watchman, steps forward on the stroke of midnight, and smashes in the groom's head with his spiked mace. With that, the clock disappears, the organ begins to play by itself, the church glows as if it were on fire, and the princess announces that she will marry the worthy young craftsman. On the other hand, the fact that the artist finally receives the recognition he deserves seems to suggest that he is, in fact, more important than his creation.

In the end, however, Andersen makes it clear that it is neither the work of art itself nor the artist who created it that should be the focus of our attention and admiration, but rather the effect of art on its audience. As the princess and the artist exchange their vows, the narrator notes, "Everyone rejoiced, everyone blessed him. There was not one person who was jealous—yes, that is the most incredible thing of all!" (408). According to the story, the most incredible thing in the world is neither an object that can be displayed nor a feat performed by an individual, but rather the stimulation of goodwill in the hearts of men. The ax-wielding brute did an incredible, awful thing when he destroyed the clock, but its only result was dismay, whereas the clock's miraculous restoration and semidivine retribution changed the hearts of all those who witnessed it. It is this three-way connection—between the artist, the artwork, and the audience—that is constantly being renewed, every time a story is read or a piece of music is heard.

Hans Christian Andersen was a great artist who wrote, among many other texts, more than 150 fairy tales, many of which are masterpieces that have entered and enriched the canon of world literature. In the fairy tale of his own life, he did not win the princess, though he did earn a king's ransom in royalties; like the merchant's son in "The Flying Trunk," he sacrificed the dream of a stable, bourgeois life for his art. He played the part of a trickster on occasion, like the professor in "The Professor and the Flea," and a visionary at other times, like the author in "The Pen and the Inkwell," but Andersen was always an artist, and his isolation and loneliness were part of the price he paid for his art. Yet more than a century after his death, the spirit of his art lives on, like the clock in "The Most Incredible Thing." Whenever people hear his stories, whether they know his name or not, whether they give him credit for the story or not, Hans Christian Andersen continues to affect the lives of people all over the world.

Works Cited

Andersen, H. C. (1983). *The Complete Fairy Tales and Stories*, translated by Erik Christian Haugaard. New York: Anchor Books.

Andersen, H.C. (2004). *Fairy Tales*, translated by Tiina Nunnally. New York: Penguin.

Heltoft, Kjeld (1977). *Hans Christian Andersen as an artist*. Copenhagen: The Royal Danish Ministry of Foreign Affairs.

Chapter V

Anxious Authors and Uncanny Shadows

Hans Christian Andersen in Dialogue with Søren Kierkegaard

Karin Sanders

In 1838, Hans Christian Andersen, by then the author of a fictional travelogue, three novels, numerous plays and poems, and his first collection of fairy tales, received a scathing and condescending review by a young Søren Kierkegaard, eight years his junior. Kierkegaard claimed that Andersen, in his third novel *Only a Fiddler*, from 1837, did not know how to create characters in a novel; they became blots of ink on the page, lacking firm contours, making it difficult for the reader to distinguish the fictional beings from their author. To Kierkegaard the novelist must be an omnipotent creator in charge of his characters: "The really talented novelist," he notes, "is able by one single oblique remark in the course of the narrative to remind the reader, as it were, so strongly of some character in the novel that he now suddenly appears once again as large as life before him and perhaps more clearly than at any time before—in short, from a single rib he is able to create the whole individual for us. Andersen is far from doing this" (Kierkegaard 1838, 90). Instead, Andersen cries over his unhappy heroes, unable to maintain the necessary distance to create believable characters. In Kierkegaard's view, it was necessary for an author to practice deception, as he himself would later do in his pseudonymous authorship. In *Point of View on My Authorship*, written in 1848 and published posthumously in 1859, Kierkegaard therefore maintains that an author must annihilate himself in order for a work to stand "on its own."

Andersen had met Kierkegaard on the streets of Copenhagen shortly after *Only a Fiddler*'s publication and Kierkegaard had told him that he planned to publish a favorable review. Evidently, the philosopher reread the novel, changed his mind, and published *From the Papers of One Still Living, Published Against His Will* in 1838, in which he not only decimates Andersen as a novelist but also brutally attacks Andersen as a person, suggesting that he was not a "real" man, but an androgynous flower engaging in self-pollination. Andersen's reaction to Kierkegaard's harsh review was, unsurprisingly, a sense of despair; in his diaries he notes that he walked as if in a coma. But years later, in his autobiography published in 1855, the same year as Kierkegaard's death, Andersen, by then a famous author, notes with the calmness of hindsight that "the Hegelian heaviness" in Kierkegaard's book made it so difficult to read that "it was said in jest that only Kierkegaard and Andersen had read the whole book [...]. At that time this is what I got out of it: that I was no writer but a fictitious character who had slipped out of his category, and that it would be the task of some future writer to put me back into it or to use me as a character in a work in which he could create a supplement to me!" (Kirmmse 1996, 28).

But Andersen had already responded in a more indirect way, two years after Kierkegaard's book was published, in the form of a dramatic satire called *A Comedy in the Open Air* (1840). Its subtitle, "an actor against his will," deliberately mimics the subtitle of Kierkegaard's critique, which read "published against his will." In Andersen's comedy, Kierkegaard is depicted as a hairdresser who speaks nonsense, regurgitating incomprehensible Hegelianism. Greatly irked, not least that Andersen misread his writings as Hegelian mimicry, Kierkegaard wrote a rebuttal called "Just a moment, Mr. Andersen," in which he complains that "the entire Andersen machination [was but] an empty gesture" and concludes: "Should Andersen wish to continue this dispute, then in order not to burden the papers with my insignificant scribbling, I would suggest to him that we publish a paper together, and in order to have nothing to reproach myself with through causing him expense, I will gladly defray the costs. ... " (Kierkegaard 1840, 222). Kierkegaard never published his rebuttal, but he had already left his mark.

This chapter will demonstrate how Andersen absorbed and reflected on Kierkegaard's critique as he continually pondered problems of authorship. He abandoned novel writing for more than a decade and concentrated on fairy tales, where he found a form that allowed for a different kind of indirect communication, or deception, than the one Kierkegaard had adopted in his work. We will see how Andersen implicitly ties anxiety of authorship to the uncanny: what does it mean to lose control of your fictional characters? What is the status of the author? How is the uncanny tied to the relationship between author, text, and reader?

Anxious Authoring

Andersen found himself both drawn to and threatened by the opportunities of print and he produced a host of meta-stories in which he contemplated the nature of writing. In a short tale from 1858, for example, called "The A-B-C Book," Andersen saw an ominous potency within the very fabric and building block of fictional worlds, the alphabet:

> What a frightful power they have! Everything depends on how they are told to stand; they can give life, kill, and create joy or sadness. On their own, they mean nothing, only when placed in formation, —indeed, when our Lord placed them under his brain waves, we fell to our knees, feeling more than *we* were able to bear, but the letters bore it. (Andersen 1858, 193, my trans.)

The terrifying power of letters gives them control over humans, because, unlike humans, they are not burdened by feelings, but can bear the heavy messages that bring humans to their knees. Their authority does not only derive from the ability to form meaning (or carry meaning projected from authors or from "above") but also from *being* substance and matter. These powers of materiality and meaning allow the alphabet to take control—but also, as Andersen suggests elsewhere—to lose control, for alphabetic letters in Andersen's world can have fits, pencils can jump in agony, and exercise books can sob.

It is clear that a manuscript's transformation into print was an anxious one for Andersen and he often identified the life of the physical object (ink, pen, paper, manuscripts, printed books, copies, and their circulation) as a potential challenge to the author's ability to control his literary creations. This much he had learned from Kierkegaard's attack: when a novel or a story took on a life of its own, separated from its place of origin, words and characters that germinated in the author's imagination were suddenly at the mercy of readers and critics and vulnerable to the cruelty of the market. A market, as Andersen was fond of repeating, that was often more interested in material value than in poetic value. Book or manuscript pages being used as wrappings for everyday commodities like green soap, fish, cheese, or foods of all sorts, therefore, represent some of Andersen's most dominant and recurring anxieties. Instead of reaching readers as anticipated through the imaginary of fiction, manuscripts and books in print were, he often repeated, submitted to the hazards of commercial materialism. Underneath Andersen's unease about the fate and future of his poetic brainchildren lies a concern about the separation of author from text. If an author did not annihilate himself, as stipulated by Kierkegaard, could he be annihilated by his own fictional creation?

Controlling Shadows

In the brilliant fairy tale "The Shadow" from 1847, we find traces of both Kierkegaard's charge that a poetic character can set itself in opposition to its author and of his harsh claim that Andersen, as a novelist, lacked control of his literary characters. The tale essentially describes a fictional being (the shadow) that is separated from its "body" of origin, then takes control of its own story, and eventually stages the killing of its author.

The author, a myopically optimistic scholar and philosopher, releases his shadow into a house across the attic from his room, a house that he presumes to be the house of poetry. After losing his shadow the learned man almost immediately starts growing a new one, like growing beard stubbles after a shave. Andersen uses this basic biological fact to illustrate to his readers that there is a difference between a real human and one that is merely dressed up and "just masquerading" as one (Andersen 1847, 233). The proof lies in the beard, so to speak; the shadow cannot grow one. If you cannot grow a beard, you cannot grow a shadow; and if you cannot grow a shadow, you are not a human, even if this particular specimen "was exceptionally well dressed, and that was exactly what made him a human being" (227). Through irony the reader is taught to be suspicious about the reality perceived.

The fate of the human in this aesthetically, existentially, and philosophically complicated fairy tale is disturbing. The thin flat shadow gradually gains a body—is fleshed out—by way of obtaining human experience: the more "it" knows of human life, the more corporeal it becomes. It grows and takes nourishment from devouring human secrets and from absorbing clandestine human actions. As a kind of reality-freak (in opposition to the world-weary theory-buff of a learned man), the shadow ultimately starts to look the part of a human and learns to speak the part of a human. But it remains an avatar, never gaining a soul. And in the end, it acts soullessly and inhumanely when it orchestrates the demise of its former master who, according to the logic of the tale, allowed this embodied (literary) being to run out of control, a cautionary lesson that Andersen had learned from Kierkegaard.

Andersen's use of shadows has roots in Plato's cave parable in *The Republic*, where we learn that shadows are second-order

Figure 5.1 Vilhelm Pedersen's classic 1847 illustration of "The Shadow."

things, seductive untruths or deceitful simulacra that cover up the ideal real. Andersen no doubt also knew of superstitions according to which a shadow represented the living dead; losing one's shadow was a warning of one's death. In fact, when Andersen's shadow returns for a first visit to its former owner, it addresses the learned man with this menacing prophecy: "A sense of longing came over me to see you again before you die. You *are* going to die, you know!" (Andersen 1847, 226).

But Andersen's interest in shadows also has roots in European Romanticism, in which shadows were given a particularly ominous inflection: they were seen as a person's double, a kind of darkness tied to the self. Already in 1814 Adelbert von Chamisso, who would later become Andersen's German translator and friend, published *The Remarkable Story of Peter Schlemihl*, which tells of a man who sold his shadow for gold only to find that lacking a shadow causes him to be shunned in human company. When the learned man in Andersen's tale discovers that his shadow had not returned, we find this tacit reference to Chamisso's story:

> He [the learned man] was annoyed, not so much because the shadow was gone but because he knew there was another story about a man without a shadow. Everyone back home in the cold countries knew about it, and if the learned man now came and told his own story, they would say that he was just copying the other one and he shouldn't bother. So he decided not to say anything about it, and that was sensible. (225)

Or perhaps not so sensible! Since we know that the failure to take control of his own story will in time come back to haunt our author, this expressed fear of plagiarism is certainly ironic. Andersen's book-learned man, we should also note, never sells his shadow (as did Chamisso's Peter Schlemihl) and so never loses *himself* in this fashion. He is lost because he is clueless and powerless vis-à-vis the all-too-human machinations of the shadow-avatar. The fact that the original dislodgement occurred at the command of the learned man only adds insult to injury.

As seen, shadows like those in Chamisso's and Andersen's tales have frequently been seen as a split of the self *within* the human, and as a result these tales often elicit psychological or existential interpretations. Still, we should not forget that in Andersen's version the corrupt shadow exhibits a far more complex sense of self-reflection than does the learned man; it knows how to *see itself*. That is, when it casts its penetrating gaze widely and deeply it takes note of *how* it is perceived, notices that people are fooled by appearances and surfaces, and uses this insight to build an identity that *looks like* human-ness. The naïve and myopic human, in contrast, is dragged like a reluctant servant after his own former shadow (just as Kierkegaard saw Andersen being dragged along by his literary beings) and ultimately succumbs to a lack of experience in actuality.

When Andersen's learned man at long last tries to set the record straight and inform the public and the princess that they have been unscrupulously deceived by a menacing avatar, his only option or strategy is, ironically, to stay with the plain *truth*: "I'll tell the

Figure 5.2 This 1866 engraving by the Dalziel brothers captures the increasing corporeality of the learned man's shadow.

whole story. That I'm a human being, and you're the shadow. That you're just masquerading" (Andersen 1847, 233). However, at this juncture in the story, words as pure bearers of truth have been seriously compromised. In fact, Andersen's shadow has developed into a con artist, able to decimate its "author" by a feat of linguistic acrobatics, namely convincing the princess (and with her, the law of the land that will carry out the execution) that the human is a shadow, the shadow a human. The groundwork for this infamous reversal is laid earlier in the tale with a puzzling exchange in which the learned man's assurance, "a man is true to his word," is countered by the shadow's mysterious response: "a word is true to its shadow" (227).

We know what it means for a man to be true to his word, but the reader is left to ponder what it means that a "word is true to its shadow." Nevertheless, the repeated twisting and falsifications of words and meanings by the shadow throughout the tale teach the reader about the shadow's specific fictitiousness; a fictitiousness build on illicit information gathered from the underbelly of the human condition: "I saw everything there was to see" (228). Instead of publishing "everything" in the newspapers, the shadow becomes a human look-alike by way of terror and distortion, by using "words" to gather an existence and grow a body.

As the shadow gains a body and grows fat, it wins the battle of agency and eventually becomes sovereign of the land *and* of the story. The book-learned man, our author, on the other hand, becomes a *shadow* of his former self; he is continually placed outside of the actuality in which the shadow immerses itself and is eventually stamped out, executed. He has lost "authorial" control of the literary being he created and, as a result, loses control of his life.

The Fantastical or the Human

To play at being human was no trivial matter for Andersen even if it permits him to expose human triviality. To him, the imperative to form human characters (as Kierkegaard called for) was more effectively tackled outside of the formalism of novel writing, just as literary production and authorial intentionality were more effectively articulated by way of that which was not human: shadows. Because they are excluded from a human code of ethics, shadows (and other non-human things), Andersen suggests, can act out more freely and enunciate more clearly (and sometimes devastatingly) their critiques of the human. In short, his simultaneously naïve and pragmatic observation of the shadow's uncanny social success and ascension to power allowed him to articulate, in the form of a fairy tale, the disassociation between author and fictional characters that he, according to Kierkegaard, was unable to constitute in his novels.

It is tempting to compare the scholar in Andersen's tale to Kierkegaard's description of a distracted Hegelian professor, who regards life from a speculative viewpoint. "A somewhat sorry figure," Kierkegaard calls such a character and goes on to describe as "fantastically in the world of abstraction, forgetting the demands of existence upon him," so that losing himself "in the world of speculation he puts his own Ego away, as one puts away his stick. ... When reading the biography of such a thinker," Kierkegaard goes on, "one sometimes shudders at the thought of what it means to be a human being" (Kierkegaard 1846, 302).

Like Kierkegaard's distracted professor, Andersen's scholar in "The Shadow" exists, but separated from actuality. He does not take upon himself the self that has been given him as *his* individual self, with the task that all humans face, according to Kierkegaard, namely to develop oneself ethically (and eventually, if you dare to leap, according to the will of God). If this development of self goes astray, it leads to "the 'fantastical' person, or the 'inhuman' person" (Brandt 1963, 78). Instead of becoming himself, the fantastical person is at the mercy of his environment; he flies where the wind blows him, succumbing to everything that happens to him. Without will and self-consciousness, that is, consciousness about self, the person loses himself. Yet, as Kierkegaard insists, if "will" becomes abstract, separated from actuality and reality, if it has no concrete attachment to actuality, it becomes insubstantial. As Kierkegaard would later elaborate in *Sickness unto Death*, in 1849, two years after Andersen published "The Shadow," a person without roots in reality becomes "fantastical" if he lacks a self: "Such things do not create much of a stir in the world, for a self is the last thing the world cares about and the most dangerous thing for a person to show signs of having. The greatest hazard of all, losing the self, can occur very quietly in the world, as if it were nothing at all" (Kierkegaard 1849, 32–33). As we can see, Andersen's doubled man/shadow and Kierkegaard's fantastical person are remarkably alike. To lose one's shadow is to lose, perhaps, one's self.

The Uncanny

Yet there are also other ways to consider the loss of one's shadow. Separations of shadows from material bodies, as Lasse Horne Kjældgaard has recently noted, was known and understood from traditional shadow theaters, but gained a new epistemological currency with the emergence of new recording technologies such as daguerreotypes and photography in the 19th century. These new visual technologies

> made it relevant to talk about the image as something that may "stick" to a person and become "detached" or even "stolen" from him or her. It introduced a new language for talking about the relation between self and image. The point of photographic pictures is that this physical connection can be broken, and the indexical sign be released from its referent and circulate and proliferate freely. (Kjældgaard 2006, 16)

Andersen's shadow, it follows, should be seen in regard to a new experience of "emancipated images" (13).

When the strong link between the man's body and the shadow has been broken, as Andersen shows in "The Shadow," the previous order of things, where man/shadow remain attached, is disrupted. This move brings a new kind of anxiety into play: *not* one that rests latently within the subject, but one that is tied to the very real experience of dislodged images (such as photographs dislodged from their source) that appear to take on lives of their own.

Seen from this perspective we find a strong reverberation of the uncanny in Andersen's "The Shadow." If we follow Sigmund Freud in his essay "The Uncanny" from 1919, fairy tales defy logic, and are therefore exempt from uncanniness. Freud, in fact, is specific on this point and insists that while fairy tales (and he singles out Andersen as an example) make striking uses of animation, they are "not in the least uncanny."

> Indeed, the fairy tale is quite openly committed to the animistic view that thoughts and wishes are all-powerful, but I cannot cite one genuine fairy story in which anything uncanny occurs. We are told that it is highly uncanny when inanimate objects—pictures or dolls—come to life, but in Hans Andersen's stories the household utensils, the furniture and the tin soldiers are alive, and perhaps nothing is further removed from the uncanny. (Freud 1919, 153)

The uncanny, rather, Freud insists, comes about when we are in doubt as to the reality we see: is it a human? Or is it a doll? A shadow? Is it alive? Or is it dead?

In fairy tales, we instinctively expect an experience of the uncanny when confronted with return-of-the-dead scenes such as those Andersen makes use of in "The Travel Companion" from 1835 where the hero, Johannes, fights off grave robbers and where the "grateful dead" returns as a traveling companion who pays back his debt by securing Johannes' fortune in wondrous ways (Johannes will ultimately marry a princess and gain a kingdom). Yet, as Freud reiterates, reanimation of the dead is "commonplace in fairy tales" (153). We need instead to be placed in a state of uncertainty, as Freud learned from his colleague Ernst Jentsch: "One of the surest devices for producing slightly uncanny effects through story-telling ... is to leave the reader wondering whether a particular figure is a real person or an automaton" (135).

Andersen's fairy tales rarely, if ever, ask his readers to imagine or experience the uncanny feeling that inanimate objects can produce if mistaken for humans. A speaking doll or pen or jackhammer in Andersen's world is rarely uncanny in this overt way. Even his use of marionettes frequently navigates free of the bewilderment (is it real or is it not?) of the uncanny—the reader is never in doubt. "The Shadow" is, however, an exception. When, for example, the learned man in "The Shadow" is executed, we are to imagine that the multitude (that is, the populace within story) is left to live in a sustained state of ignorance

THE PRINCESS AND THE SHADOW STEPPED OUT UPON THE BALCONY TO SHOW THEMSELVES,
AND TO HEAR THE PEOPLE SHOUT "HURRAH!" ONCE MORE.

Figure 5.3 Hans Tegner's illustration from 1900 shows the princess and the shadow being applauded by the crowd while the learned man is being put to death.

that *is* positively uncanny. *They* do not know what *we* know, namely that their new sovereign is not human. Only the learned man knew the nature of the shadow, but he is dead. Yet, of course, the reader knows. At the conclusion of the tale, therefore, the effect of the uncanny rests solely with the reader. If the princess sees the execution of the learned man as an act of humanity facilitated by her fiancé, the shadow, the reader in turn is meant to shudder at the inhumanity of it all.

As mentioned above, Kierkegaard insisted that an author must annihilate himself. Andersen, perhaps as a circuitous response, offers us a tale in which an author is indeed annihilated by his "self" in form of his shadow. Andersen's indirect communication with

Kierkegaard took in 1848 a more direct turn as Andersen sent Kierkegaard a copy of his *New Fairy Tales* signed "the author." Knowing what we now know about Andersen's struggle with an author's authority over his fictional creations, his dedication is worth quoting in full, which also allows us to give our fairy tale author the last word: "Dear Mr. Kirkegaard [*sic*], *Either* [i.e., whether] you like my little ones *Or* you do not like them, they come without *Fear* and *Trembling*, and that in itself is something. Sincerely, the Author" (Wullschlager 2001, 182).

Works Cited

Andersen, H. C. (2000). [1855] *The Fairy Tale of My Life. An Autobiography*, translated by Naomi Lewis. New York: Cooper Square Press.

Andersen, H. C. (2003). [1858] "ABC-Bogen" [The A-B-C-Book]. In *Hans Christian Andersen Samlede Værker*, Vol. II, edited by Klaus P. Mortensen. Det danske sprog- og litteraturselskab. Copenhagen: Gyldendal.

Andersen, H. C. (2005). [1847] "The Shadow." In *Fairy Tales*, translated by Tiina Nunnally. New York: Viking Penguin.

Brandt, Frithiof (1963). *Søren Kierkegaard 1813–1855: His Life, His Works*, translated by Ann R. Born. Copenhagen: Det Danske Selskab.

Freud, Sigmund (2003). [1919] *The Uncanny*, translated by David Mclintock. London: Penguin.

Kierkegaard, Søren (1990). [1838] *From the Papers of One Still Living*. In *Early Polemical Writings. Kierkegaard Writings*, I, edited and translated by Julia Watkins. Princeton, NJ: Princeton University Press.

Kierkegaard, S. (1990). [1840] "Et Øjeblik, Hr Andersen." In *Early Polemical Writings. Kierkegaard Writings*, I, edited and translated by Julia Watkins. Princeton, NJ: Princeton University Press.

Kierkegaard, S. (1992). [1846] *Concluding Unscientific Postscript*, translated by Howard V. Hong and Edna H. Hong. Princeton, NJ: Princeton University Press.

Kierkegaard, S. (1980). [1849] *Sickness unto Death*, translated by Howard V. Hong and Edna H. Hong. Princeton, NJ: Princeton University Press.

Kierkegaard, S. (2009). [1848/1859] *Point of View on My Authorship*, translated by Howard V. Hong and Edna H. Hong. Princeton, NJ: Princeton University Press.

Kirmmse, B. (1996). *Encounters with Kierkegaard. A Life as Seen by His Contemporaries*. Princeton, NJ: Princeton University Press.

Kjældgaard, L. H. (2006). *The Emancipation of Images. The Optical Unconscious of Hans Christian Andersen's "The Shadow."* Romantikselskabets skriftserie, Nr. 44, edited by M. Nygaard. Copenhagen: Dansk Selskab for Romantikstudier.

Wullschlager, J. (2001). *Hans Christian Andersen. The Life of a Storyteller*. New York: Alfred A. Knopf.

Chapter VI

"I can fly up into the everlasting light, the eternal glory!"

The Role of Religion in Hans Christian Andersen's Fairy Tales

Julie K. Allen

When we think of fairy tales, we tend to focus on quest narratives, talking animals, and magical gifts, but we often forget that the fairy tale tradition is also a highly didactic one. In addition to their wondrous elements, fairy tales and folktales tend to offer cautionary lessons and moral instruction, which are generally framed in terms of the Christian theology that was ubiquitous in Europe at the time of their composition. As a product of 19th-century European society and a pioneer in the establishment of the literary fairy tale as a genre, Hans Christian Andersen could hardly have avoided being influenced by the religious climate of his time, but, as we'll see in this chapter, although he frequently includes moralizing messages in his tales, his treatment of religion is far more nuanced than a simple restatement of mainstream Christian views.

It is difficult to overstate the centrality of religion in the lives of ordinary people in Denmark in the early 19th century. For more than a thousand years, the kingdom of Denmark has been officially Christian. For most of that time, from King Harald Bluetooth's decision in the tenth century to convert to Christianity until the establishment of religious freedom in the Danish constitution of 1849, citizens of Denmark had virtually no choice in the matter of their own religious beliefs or affiliation. Even when the Protestant Reformation swept across Europe in the 16th century and proclaimed the importance of the common man's access to biblical truth, Denmark's conversion from Catholicism to Lutheranism was a top-down phenomenon driven by King Frederick II's personal convictions and political calculations, not a reflection of the desires and will of the Danish people.

By the time the boy who would one day become the famous author Hans Christian Andersen was born in Odense, Denmark, in 1805, Lutheranism was an integral part of the fabric of everyday life for Danes. The parish priest was both a spiritual shepherd and a government official, in charge of taking the census and enforcing the rule of law. Church attendance was mandatory, but private meetings to discuss theology were forbidden. Like nearly all of his peers, Andersen was baptized as an infant and confirmed as a member of the Danish Lutheran church as an adolescent, around the age of 14. These rituals were designed to ensure that all Danish children were raised to believe in Lutheran theology, so that they would become faithful, obedient citizens of both God and the king. To a certain extent, one could say that Danish Lutheranism in the early 1800s was more concerned with maintaining public order than with fostering spiritual growth.

Yet the 19th century was also a time of tremendous social and political change in Denmark that destabilized this long-standing state of affairs by introducing the element of individual choice in religious matters. In the early decades of the century, during Andersen's childhood and youth, lay preachers held illegal private meetings across the country, preaching a fervently devout brand of Christian pietism that emphasized the suffering of Christ and the individual believer's emotional connection to God. These religious meetings also had a political dimension that promoted the rise of democracy in Denmark and led to the shift from an absolute to a constitutional monarchy in 1848, as well as the establishment of a range of civil rights, including freedom of religion, in 1849. Although the unity of the Danish church and the Danish state remains legally intact to this day, the relationship between the average Dane and religion underwent a fundamental change during Andersen's lifetime.

This tension between Christian tradition and secularism manifested itself in Andersen's own life. Raised by a devout but uneducated mother and a religiously skeptical father, Andersen was prone to doubts about religion and rarely went to church, although he retained a strong sense of personal spirituality into adulthood. He was uninterested in theological orthodoxy, describing in his diary, on June 13, 1870, an argument with his fellow houseguests at the Basnæs estate: "Since I didn't believe in the Father, the Son, and the Holy Ghost, I wasn't a Christian. I answered that I believed in them as concepts but not as people, corporeal beings. They almost gave up on me ..." (Wullschlager 2004, xxxix). For Andersen, religion was not a matter of dogma but of emotion, a position that aligned with the radical pietism that was prevalent throughout Denmark, especially in rural areas, in the early decades of the 19th century.

Given this historical context, it should come as no surprise that many of Andersen's stories reflect the tumultuous religious climate of 19th-century Denmark. On one hand, the values and practices of Lutheran Christianity appear in many tales, from the biblical reference implicit in "The Garden of Eden," the ritual of confirmation in "The Bell," and the humble acknowledgment of the majesty of God in "The Pen and the Inkwell," to the condemnation of vanity and pride in "The Red Shoes." On the other hand, Andersen's articulation of Christian theology does not conform strictly to Lutheranism or any other organized religion, consisting instead of a hodgepodge of symbols and moral messages. Andersen's literary treatment of religion is not, in fact, particularly Christian at all, but is quite universalist in its affirmation of the power of God, the need for humility and compassion, and the possibility of transcendence for all, regardless of social status. In this chapter, we'll look closely at two clusters of tales—"The Story of a Mother" and "The Dead Child," followed by "On the Last Day," "The Angel," and "The Old Oak Tree's Last Dream"— in order to explore how Andersen uses religion as a plot device, a vehicle for social criticism, and a stimulus for existential self-examination.

Before we dive into the analysis of the tales themselves, however, it may be worthwhile to define the terminology we'll be employing, in particular the distinction between religious motifs and themes. A motif is simply a reference, often recurring, to a person, place, thing, concept, or event. Motifs do not generally dictate the course or tone of a given tale, but they are used in a meaningful way, often for their symbolic associations. In this manner, religious motifs function as a kind of literary shorthand for evoking specific ideas, beliefs, customs, or traditions. In his tales, Andersen incorporates religious motifs from many different belief systems, including Greek and Roman mythology, Judaism, Islam, Catholicism, animism, and Protestant Christianity. An attentive reader will discover religious motifs such as Amor, Allah, Ahasverus the wandering Jew, astrology, angels, and the afterlife, just to start at the beginning of the alphabet.

While motifs are useful and important, we will be focusing primarily on religious themes in Andersen's tales. In contrast to a motif, a theme is the central idea or message of a text. Themes are much broader and more complex than motifs, but motifs can help develop a theme. The religious themes in Andersen's tales tend to explore the conditions of human life in relation to the divine or the absolute, and to affirm or condemn certain values and characteristics. One religious theme that recurs frequently in Andersen's tales is the importance of *agape*, which is a Greek term meaning selfless love, such as the love of a parent for a child. Since the Greek New Testament uses *agape* to denote God's love for humankind, for example in John 3:16, it has acquired a specifically Christian connotation. This theme appears in several of Andersen's tales, often as a positive ideal that is contrasted with a character's self-destructive negative behavior, such as the selfishness and pride that drive little Inger, the protagonist of "The Girl Who Stepped on Bread," to prioritize her appearance above concern for her poverty-stricken parents when she casts the loaf of bread she is bringing home to them into the mud to protect her shoes as she crosses a puddle. The selfless compassion of a pure-hearted woman eventually redeems Inger from her excruciating punishment in hell, but she has to earn her own salvation through selfless service to others, a demonstration of *agape*. In the following, we will explore two additional modes by which Andersen explores the connection between *agape* and religion in his tales.

In the Hand of God: "The Story of a Mother" (1848) and "The Dead Child" (1859)

The first two tales we will look at deal with religiously informed responses to the loss of a loved one. One of the weightiest questions that religions strive to answer is why God allows people to suffer. Some Eastern religions such as Jainism attribute suffering to the sufferer's greed and hatred in a past life, while medieval European Christians tended to look for the cause of suffering in the victim's (mis)behavior in this life. The answer to this question that Andersen offers in his tale "The Story of a Mother" is at once more comforting and yet stark: that some suffering is necessary to prevent greater suffering and as a reminder to trust God's wisdom. The tale, which was first published as a Christmas book in London in 1847, opens with a woman watching over her very ill child, who poses this question to the poor old man to whom she has given shelter from the winter night: "'You think I'll be allowed to keep him, don't you?' she said. 'Surely Our Lord wouldn't take him from me?'" (Andersen 2004, 253). There is no discussion of sin or guilt, just the poignant hope that God, being merciful, would not deprive a woman of her beloved child.

Figure 6.1 Alfred Walter Bayes' 1866 illustration of "The Story of a Mother" captures the mother's hope that her child will recover.

Yet the pervasiveness of religious belief in 19th-century Denmark did not result in low rates of child mortality. Attendance at Sunday church services was mandatory in Denmark until 1849, but one in five children did not reach their fifth birthday (Wullschlager 2004, 433). Given the dearth of medical resources available at the time, religion provided the only solace for grieving parents, asserting that a child's death was an expression of God's will and nurturing hope in an afterlife, where parents could hope to see their child again. Andersen's tale takes up these well-worn themes and explores how such assurances relate to the pain of loss that a parent would feel in such a situation.

After the mother has posed her question, the narrator informs us that the old man, "who was Death himself, nodded so strangely; it could just as well mean yes as no" (Andersen 2004, 253). This ambiguous response offers little comfort to the exhausted, despairing mother, who "looked down at her lap and the tears ran down her cheeks" (253), but it sets up the quest that takes up the bulk of the story, for Death has come, of course, to take the child. The mother falls asleep for a moment, and when she wakes with a start, "the old man was gone and her little child was gone too. He had taken the child with him and over in the corner the old clock was whirring and whirring. The big lead weight plunged all the way down to the floor: Bam! And the clock too stood still" (253). It was the custom at the time to stop clocks and cover mirrors when someone died in a house; Andersen causes the clock to stop on its own as a consequence of the child's sudden absence from his home, but the mother refuses to believe that her child is dead and runs out into the snow, calling for him.

The mother's reaction to her child's apparent death can be interpreted as a manifestation of her faith that God would not, in fact, rob her of her child, that the old man's nod had meant "yes." She sorrows but does not grieve as she sets out to find her child, driven by her faith in God's mercy. Her religious convictions thus serve to advance the plot of the story, rendering surmountable each obstacle that she encounters. She races after Death, sacrificing her songs and tears, her heart's blood, her eyes, and her long, black hair in her quest to recover her child. She knows that her task is impossible, but she believes in the possibility of a miracle, just as Jesus Christ raised his friend Lazarus and Jairus's daughter from the dead. Andersen doesn't make an explicit biblical allusion, but simply illustrates the kind of faith that justified such divine interventions. "Oh, I would give anything to reach my child!" the mother weeps, as she literally cries her eyes out and they sink to the bottom of the lake she cannot drink dry to get across.

At first, it seems that the mother's faith will be rewarded with the successful retrieval of her child, for the lake carries her over to the immense hothouse of souls so that she arrives before Death himself, although he "moves faster than the wind, and he never brings back what he takes" (254). When challenged by the old woman who tends the soul plants, she attributes her success to God's assistance: "'Our Lord helped me,' she said. 'He is merciful, and you will be too'" (255). Despite her blindness, she recognizes the beat of her own child's heart among the millions growing in the hothouse. When Death arrives, she confronts him and demands her child back; Death warns her, "There's nothing you can do to me," but she replies with confidence, "But Our Lord can" (256). Throughout her travails, despite the wretched condition of her son's drooping flower, she stands firm in her faith that God will be merciful and spare her child from death.

This interchange marks the turning point in the story, however, for Death reminds the mother that no one can command God, not even Death himself. "'I merely do His will,' said

Death. 'I am His gardener. I take all His flowers and trees and plant them in the great garden of Paradise in the unknown land'" (256). The mother tries to force Death to give her back her child by threatening to tear up other flowers, but the selfless love that has characterized all of her actions thus far now prevents her from carrying out her threat, once she learns that doing so would rob other mothers of their children. Her inability to determine whether her child's future would have been beneficial or detrimental to the world persuades her that her faith has been misplaced: She must not trust that God will do as she desires, but that He will do what is best for her child. Her love for her child must be selfless, like God's love, or *agape*. In terror at the possibility of the misery her child's future might hold, she screams, "Save my child from all that misery! Better to take him away. Take him to God's kingdom. Forget my tears, forget my pleas and everything I've said and done" (257). To drive the point home, Death asks her to explicitly retract her demand for her child, and she "wrung her hands, fell to her knees, and prayed to Our Lord, 'Don't listen when I plead against Your will, for Your will is best! Don't listen to me! Don't listen to me!' She bowed her head to her lap. And Death took her child into the unknown land" (257).[1]

On one level, this story offers comfort that God is mindful of all people, and that death is just a movement from this life into a presumably better one, though that must be taken on faith. Death is shown to be a journey that leads to renewal, a view that affirms the goodness and wisdom of God. Yet, on another level, it asserts the impossibility of contesting God's will and the necessity of humbling oneself before Him. In the original manuscript version of the tale, Andersen allows the mother to awaken from the nightmare of having lost her child to find him restored to health (Wullschlager 2004, 434). In the final, published version, however, Andersen articulates a harsher theology of spiritual refinement through submission to the will of God. All of the mother's sacrifices and suffering are in vain, in the sense that she fails in her quest to reclaim her child, though Death does restore her eyes. Her faith that God would not allow her to suffer the loss of her child proves to be misplaced. But instead of cursing God and losing her faith, the mother renews it, trusting that her suffering will be the means of protecting her son.

The theme of purification through suffering and submission that characterizes "The Story of a Mother" appears again in another of Andersen's somewhat later tales, "The Dead Child" (1859). The premise of the tale is similar, involving a mother who loses her young son, but her reaction is opposite to that of the mother in the earlier tale. This mother also asks how God could take her child from her, but the fact of his death causes her to "let go of God; and dark thoughts came, thoughts about eternal death—that all was over when our bodies became dust in the dust. With such thoughts, she could hold onto nothing, and she fell into the deepest despair" (Andersen 1983, 642). Instead of trusting in God's mercy, the mother succumbs to depression, neglecting her husband and her living

---

1   This designation echoes Shakespeare's Hamlet, who describes the afterlife in his famous soliloquy as "the undiscovered country from whose bourn/no traveler returns" (*Hamlet*, Act III, Scene I).

children. "All her thoughts were with her dead child," but the reader soon learns that her obsession with him is selfish rather than an expression of *agape*: "She had abandoned herself to her grief; she was floundering now in a dark ocean, like a ship that has lost its rudder" (642). In contrast to the mother who is able to accomplish the impossible task of beating Death back to his own garden, this mother cannot do anything but dream of her lost son.

But although Death in "The Story of a Mother" refuses to disclose any information about the afterlife, he offers the mother in "The Dead Child" the chance to go down into the grave to be with her child, much like Orpheus descends into Hades to find his love, Eurydice, in the

Figure 6.2 "The Mother at the Grave" (1866) by Alfred Walter Bayes shows the mother's desperation at the loss of her child.

Greek myth. Reunited with her son, she "pressed him to her heart ... [and] shouted for joy," covering him with kisses (644), but her pleasure in their reunion is spoiled when her son chastises her, both for neglecting his sisters and for holding him back from flying "together with all the other happy children, right up to God. I would like to so much, but your tears hold me back. When you weep I cannot leave you, and I want to. Please let me go, may I? After all, it is but so short a time, and then you will be with me" (645). The mother suddenly realizes that her obsessive, selfish love is the obstacle preventing her child from experiencing the bliss of God's presence, as well as a source of distress for her remaining family.

As in the previous story, the mother humbles herself before God and renews her faith in Him, though at the cost of her own desires. This type of sober self-denial is a familiar trope from Christian theology, but Andersen employs it not only for its theological merits, but also as a means of resolving the tension within the tale. When the mother wakes from her dream of visiting the underworld, she prays, "Forgive me, Lord, that I would keep a soul from its flight toward you, and forgive me for forgetting my duties toward the living" (645). In accepting the will of God, she surrenders her own will, reaffirms her commitment to living a Christian life, and finds peace in her heart. Out of her suffering comes strength, which "she found in the belief that God's will is always for the best" (645), and the family's (and by extension, society's) equilibrium is restored.

Face to Face with God: "On the Last Day" (1852), "The Angel" (1843), and "The Old Oak Tree's Last Dream" (1857)

The tales in the second group we'll consider turn inward to explore the religious individual's reaction to his or her own death and resulting confrontation with the divine. Unlike the first two tales we examined, which generally affirm a dogmatic Christian theology of self-denial and suffering, these tales call into question the self-congratulatory exclusivity of that same mainstream Christianity, which was the state religion in Denmark during Andersen's lifetime, and challenge the reader to conceive of a more inclusive, nonjudgmental God by celebrating the possibility of universal salvation.

The tale "On the Last Day" is set precisely at the moment of death, which is described as a transcendental moment: "The most sacred of all the days of our life is the day we die. It is holy, it is the great day of change, of transformation" (Andersen 1983, 401). This occasion provides the impetus for self-examination, as the narrator asks: "Have you ever seriously thought about the hour that is certain to come and will be your last hour on earth?" When the protagonist dies, his soul follows the angel of Death with confidence, secure in the knowledge that he has been "'strong in the faith,' as they say. He was a warrior for God and His Word, a zealous servant of a zealous God" (401). And yet, although his "life had been guided by the strictest religious doctrines," he soon discovers that he is not as righteous as he believed himself to be. In the masquerade of humanity, he sees himself as a peacock, and is pained to recognize his own evil thoughts, evil desires, and thoughtless words. At the gates of heaven, the angel asks him who he is, but rejects his self-identification as a Christian with the explanation, "That I would not have guessed either from your faith or from your deeds. Christ teaches redemption, love, and mercy" (403).

Although it deals with the Day of Judgment, this tale is not concerned with depicting the wrath of a vengeful God, but rather the individual's process of self-recognition. The gates of heaven open for the man, despite his flaws, but he does not dare enter until he finally feels and understands "the burden of his own arrogance, hardness, and sin" and confesses, "What good I did in the world I did because I could not do otherwise, but the evil—that I chose to do myself" (404). Blinded by the light of heaven, the dead man's soul is still too weak and timid to enter—"He remembered his own belief in God's justice and righteousness and did not dare to beg for mercy"—but is redeemed by "God's grace, His unexpected mercy" (404). Once his pride has been crushed, his false conviction stripped away that it was God's will that he persecute nonbelievers and those who had sinned, the man is able to receive grace and mercy. The angels sing, "Holy, glorious, loving, and eternal is the human soul," and the narrator concludes:

> Every one of us will on the last day and hour of life here on earth draw back in fear and humility from the glory and splendor of heaven. We will fall; but His grace will support us and our souls will fly in new orbits, nearer and nearer the eternal light, His mercy will give us the strength to understand the final, godly, eternal wisdom. (404) While this tale overturns the notion that people can earn salvation on their own merits, it

also imposes conditions for receiving God's mercy, most importantly recognition of one's sinfulness and weakness. The message seems to be that mercy is in God's gift and does not coincide with worldly standards of accomplishment and importance.

This message is reinforced and expanded upon in "The Angel," which starts at the same moment of death, when an angel collects the soul of the person who has died, but it depicts a very different experience of judgment and salvation. In this case, the dead person is not a self-confident adult who has taken it upon himself to interpret God's will according to his own prejudiced views. Instead, it is an innocent child, who is completely free of the pride and self-importance that were such a burden to the protagonist of "On the Last Day." The angel instructs the child to pick "a whole armful of flowers and bring them to God," but instead of choosing the most elegant, perfect blossoms, the selfless child selects imperfect ones, including "a tall rosebush whose stem some evil hand had broken, so that all the branches, with their half-open buds that had already begun to wither, lay all around it," as well as wild pansies and violets. Although they have enough flowers to take up to God, the angel detours to collect a "dried-out wild flower, to whose roots a clump of soil still clung.

It had been thrown out in the street together with the other trash" (Andersen 1983, 201). The angel tells the child that this flower had been the prized possession of a sickly child who lived in a dark cellar, "his treasure on this earth. … It bloomed for him alone: to give pleasure to his eyes and send sweet fragrance for him to enjoy. When God called him, the boy turned in death toward the flower" (201). The angel reveals that he had been that ailing child. The dead child too is transformed, as is the wildflower, which God kisses, thereby giving it a voice to sing with the angels. The narrator explains, "All sang with equal bliss and fervor: those who had died when old and those who had come as children, and the little wild flower that had been thrown out among the trash in the dark and narrow lane" (202). All of them are alike unto God and share equally in His glory.

This message of universalism and tolerance may be common in today's highly secular and ecumenical Western

Figure 6.3 This illustration of "The Angel" is from a German edition of Andersen's tales.

societies, but it was by no means accepted dogma in the mid-19th century. While the Bishop of Zealand, J. P. Mynster (1775–1854), advocated for a "capacious church" with the capacity to encompass and welcome a variety of religious orientations, his tolerance did not extend to Catholics or Muslims. Even the Danish religious reformer N. F. S. Grundtvig (1783–1872) supported the right of priests to deny communion to members of the congregation he deemed "unworthy" (Rasmussen 2009, 155).

The final tale we'll examine, "The Old Oak Tree's Last Dream," builds on and intensifies the inclusivity and universality suggested in "The Angel," reinforcing the emphasis on *agape* as the core of Andersen's religious worldview. The conversation between the oak tree and the mayfly at the beginning of the tale establishes the equality between the long-lived, massive tree and the tiny, short-lived insect. Although the tree pities the mayfly for the brevity of its life, the mayfly disagrees: "You live thousands of my days, but I have thousands of moments to be happy in. ... Well there, you see, we live equally long; it is just our ways of figuring that are different" (Andersen 1983, 546).

Like "The Story of a Mother," "The Old Oak Tree's Last Dream" was intended as a Christmas story, as its subtitle informs us. The references to Christmas are a motif that alerts readers to the likelihood of the tale's religious theme, which is confirmed by the narrator's description of the "sound of the sailors singing a carol about the joyful season, when Christ was born to save mankind and give us eternal life" (549). The story is set on Christmas Eve, which, along with Easter, is one of the high points of the Christian liturgical year. Despite its strong Christian associations, however, the coincidence of the Christmas season with the winter solstice—highly significant in pagan belief systems as a celebration of the return of the sun and the rebirth of nature—invests the tale with an additional layer of religious meaning.

The Christian tradition of decorating trees at Christmas is also derived from pagan reverence for trees as a source of life and power. While evergreen trees are popular for Christmas trees and are often interpreted as symbols of Christ, oak trees have been held sacred by many cultures, due to their size, strength, and longevity, a connection that Andersen hints at with the mention of a Druid feast of thanksgiving near the end of the tale. The Germanic tribes who settled much of western Europe associated oak trees with the cult of the god of the sky (Davidson 1996, 110). According to Norse mythology, the universe is held together by the mighty ash tree called Yggdrasil, or the World Tree, where the god Odin, the All-Father, hung for nine days and nights to gain secret knowledge of magic runes (46). Yggdrasil was believed to stand at the center of the world, linking heaven and earth and connecting the realm of the gods with the world of men and the realm of the dead.

The old oak tree in Andersen's tale also connects heaven and earth. It is the tallest tree in the forest, its crown towers above all others, and birds perch in its branches. In its great age, it links generations of humanity together over the centuries. In its dream, the tree recalls everything it has seen over the course of its long life, from knights and ladies to colorful butterflies. Reviewing the panorama of its life has a transformative effect on the tree, so that it literally spans the sky:

From its tiniest root, deep down in the ground, to its topmost little twigs, it experienced an awareness of life and growth. It felt its strength increase, it was growing taller and taller. Its great crown was now enormous. As it grew, its feelings of happiness became more and more intense, and it had such a great longing for the sun that it wanted to grow right up into that golden warm sphere. In its dream, the tree had grown so tall that its top branches were above the clouds; flocks of birds were flying below them; even the swans could not fly above its crown. (Andersen 1983, 547)

Gazing out at the stars, with every leaf transformed into an eye, the oak tree enjoys a godlike perspective on the universe. In this moment of its greatness, the tree does not feel pride in itself, but rather a "longing for other trees and the bushes that grew far below it. It wished that they, too—as well as the little flowers and herbs—could lift themselves high up in the sky as it was doing and experience its joy" (548).

The tree's overpowering feeling of selfless love for all creatures is a powerful illustration of *agape*: "It felt that unless everyone took part in this great dream of happiness it would not be complete" (548). In the transcendent moment of its exaltation, the tree reaches out to every living thing around it, lifting not only the other trees, bushes, and flowers, but also the reeds from the swamp, birds, beetles, grasshoppers, and other insects. Like God, who sees every sparrow's fall, according to the book of Matthew in the New Testament, the oak tree watches out for every little flower—the "little blue flowers from the pond," the red harebell, little primrose, the "woodruff from last summer and all the lilies of the valley

IT WAS JUST ABOUT CHRISTMAS TIME THAT THE TREE DREAMED A DREAM.

Figure 6.4 This 1889 engraving of "The Last Dream of the Old Oak Tree" captures the majesty of the great tree.

from the summer before that"—"the old oak did not want anyone to be forgotten" (438). This insistence on the universality of salvation, on the impossibility of true exaltation without the inclusion of all creatures, was a radical position for Andersen to take at the time, but it exemplifies the fullest expression of the type of divine, self-sacrificing love that he so often endorses in his tales.

The spiritual ecstasy that the tree feels as it strives upward toward heaven also facilitates the narrative climax of the story, toward which the tale has been consistently building, and sets up the tale's message. The increasingly rapid exchanges between the tree and its companions speed up the pace of the story, while the proliferation of exclamation points lends urgency to its tone. As the voices of all creation sing that such happiness as the tree is feeling is possible in heaven, the tree feels its roots leave the group and cries out ecstatically, "Now no bands hold me down. I can fly up into the everlasting light, the eternal glory! And all that I held dear is with me. None has been forgotten, all are here with me, all!" (549). The narrator offers a prosaic alternative to the religious fervor articulated by the tree, informing the reader that the tree's roots did indeed leave the ground at just this moment, when it was torn up by a great storm. Similarly, the sailors in the harbor, unaware of the tree's transcendent experience, marvel at the fall of the tree in the storm and wonder how to replace their landmark. However, the juxtaposition of that mundane explanation with the Christmas carol they are singing, with the note that "the sailors were singing of the same dream, the beautiful dream that the old oak tree had dreamed Christmas Eve" (459), functions like a wink from the narrator to reassure readers that we are in on the secret of what really happened to the mighty old oak tree.

Religion appears in Andersen's fairy tales in many different guises and themes. Despite—or perhaps because of—his religious doubts, Andersen explores religion in many different tales and in widely divergent ways, sometimes harshly, other times sentimentally, and still others mystically. In this chapter, we've explored a few of Andersen's varied treatments of the theme of *agape* or divine, selfless love, but even within that narrow category, no two tales deal with religion in exactly the same way, though there are often similarities between certain aspects of multiple tales. While it can be very useful to identify religious motifs that appear in Andersen's texts, it is through identifying and analyzing the religious themes of his tales that we can begin to discern not only Andersen's own views about religion, but also our own responses to the kinds of perennial existential questions that gave rise to religion in the first place.

Works Cited

Andersen, H.C. (1983). *The Complete Fairy Tales and Stories*, translated by Erik Christian Haugaard. New York: Anchor Books..

Andersen, H.C. (2004). *Fairy Tales*, translated by Tiina Nunnally. New York: Penguin.

Davidson, H. R. E. (1996). *Viking & Norse Mythology*. New York: Barnes & Noble Books.

Rasmussen, J. (2009). *Religionstolerance og religionsfrihed. Forudsætninger og Grundloven i 1849.* Odense: Syddansk Universitetsforlag.

Wullschlager, J. (2004). "Introduction." *Fairy Tales*, by Hans Christian Andersen, xv–xlvi. New York: Penguin.

Chapter VII

Hans Christian Andersen and the City

Jakob Stougaard-Nielsen

In "A Drop of Water" (1847), Hans Christian Andersen shows us what a 19th-century city might look like if viewed through a drop of water. The story also exemplifies the genre that made Andersen a celebrity throughout the world: the literary fairy tale. The tale blends folkloric characters, a preoccupation with visual technologies, science, and urban life. An old man known by the name Wiggle-waggle is looking through his magnifying glass at a drop of ditch water. It is revealed to the reader that he is not just any old man. He has access to magical concoctions such as witch's blood, which he applies to the drop of water better to see the *infusoria* (a 19th-century term for small aquatic creatures) and in an attempt to bring order to the "revolting sight" of these tiny animals who are "hopping, jumping, pulling, pushing, and eating each other up" (Andersen 1983, 354). Like a scientist, Wiggle-waggle (whom we later infer is a troll) wants to order the world he observes, but unlike a scientist, he also wants to improve upon a world he finds so "revolting." However, the witch's blood does not change the behavior of the animals for the better. Instead, the magical blood turns the drop of water into a reflection of the urban world of humans: "They looked like a whole town of savages" (354). In other words, the witch's blood brings about a magical transformation of the unfamiliar and invisible world of the water into a familiar, urban world of humans, much in the same way a storyteller uses words and rhetorical figures to make an abstract story-world seem eerily familiar and comprehensible to his audience.

The magical, or literary transformation of the natural world in the tale allows us to see that life in a drop of water may be seen as a parable for modern life in the city. Both in the world of the water and in the city, it is a crowded and ferocious life—if, that is, we are to believe the opinion of trolls. However, in this tale, the trolls are ironically very human and modern characters: they have troll-like names such as Wiggle-waggle, but they also enjoy the civilized company of their fellows; they use magnifying glasses and engage in the very human cognitive activity of projecting their own experiences into an abstract or foreign world—an activity we engage in, for instance, when we interpret a parable or other figures of speech (Turner 1997, 5). This latter human quality of the trolls is introduced with the second troll, who is invited to peer through Wiggle-waggle's magnifying glass. While the onomatopoeic name of the first troll ironically connects him to the world of the water drop he observes, the other troll, "who had no name," is the representative of the anonymous readers of Andersen's tale. This is suggested by the fact that he, like the reader, is invited to peer through the magnifying glass and wonder at the similarity between the drop of water and the city, to make the connection between our world and the abstract world of *infusoria*. The trolls in this tale are, therefore, like the drop of water in that they represent both the wild, unfamiliar natural world and the modern, urban world of humans.

Not knowing what to expect to see through the magnifying glass, the second troll only sees the magically or artistically transformed world of the drop of water:

> What he saw looked like a city with all the inhabitants running around naked. It was a disgusting sight, but even more disgusting to see was the way people behaved. They kicked and cuffed each other; they beat and bit and shoved; those who were on the bottom strove to get to the top, and those on the top struggled to be on the bottom. (Andersen 1983, 355)

While the second troll finds the social scene in the water disgusting, he also finds it "instructive and amusing." It is worth noting, however, that the Danish phrase *overordentligt morsomt* (commonly translated as "amusing") could, in the 19th century, also be used to express something peculiar, ridiculous, or unfamiliar, instead of suggesting hilarity. Rather than filling the viewer (and the reader) with indignation or fear, the social reality of urban life, as seen through the magnifying glass (and a fairy tale), is but a mere spectacle, something to wonder at, both a familiar and at the same time radically uncanny sight.

The punch line of this little story comes after the unnamed troll provides his answer to Wiggle-waggle's riddle by confirming the figurative reading made possible by his magic: "It's Copenhagen or some other big city, they are all alike" (355). Wiggle-waggle can now reveal what the reader has known all along, that "it's ditch water!" At first sight, the tale is a mere hermeneutic joke: Seen through a magnifying glass, the scene may *appear* as a city, but it *is* really a drop of water. However, despite the narrator's ironic tone and the tale's untrustworthy trolls, the tale still invites us to consider the peculiarity and uncanny nature of life in the modern city, though we necessarily have to keep in mind that the optics through which we regard the urban scene may be a splinter from a troll's mirror (as in Andersen's "The Snow Queen") that distorts our vision and makes everything ugly. In other words, it is both a tale about the terrors of the overcrowded city in the middle of the 19th century, and a tale about observing urban life through the distorted lens of an uncanny fairy tale.

In Andersen's hands, the fairy tale as a genre is not a stranger to modern experiences and concerns. Andersen could turn just about anything into a tale, and in "A Drop of Water," which he dedicated to his friend, the Danish scientist H. C. Ørsted, he demonstrated that with an attuned poetic vision resembling the scientist's magnifying glass, the artist, or the *Seer* (as he referred to the poet in the travelogue *In Sweden*), may find beauty and poetry in the most prosaic details of everyday life. While the tale on the one hand may be considered a celebration of the power of science and the poetic imagination to reveal the hidden nature beneath the visible, on the other, it shows that the closer we look, the stranger our world will appear.

The tale also contains a biographical element, as it presents Andersen's own experiences in London in 1847, the largest, busiest, and most polluted metropolis in 19th-century Europe. In his diary from London, we see Andersen marveling at the crowded streets, the unfamiliar urban characters, the incessant traffic, advertisement posters, and the shops illuminated by gaslights (at the time, gaslights had not yet been introduced in Copenhagen). In fact, the tale was first published in English in the collection of tales entitled, *A Christmas Greeting to my English Friends* (1847), which suggests that it was written with his experiences in London fresh in his mind.

Another aspect that locates the tale in Andersen's contemporary culture is the fact that microscopes, magnifying glasses, and the mysterious, if not outright dangerous, world of urban waterways were fashionable entertainments and preoccupations of the time. Andersen had ample opportunities to learn about the creatures that live in a drop of water from his scientist friends and contemporary science books (in fact, he relates his experience of looking at a drop of water through a microscope in a letter as early as in 1830). The hidden life in urban waterways was also a popular motif for prints that circulated in the first half of the 19th century, particularly in England, where the environmental impact of urbanization came to a head in the 1840s and 1850s, when the pollution of the Thames by sewage resulted in deadly cholera and typhoid epidemics. Andersen's tale illustrates a widespread fear common to polluted and congested European metropolises of the 19th century, which was captured in popular prints such as an 1828 etching by William Heath

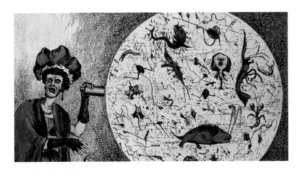

Figure 7.1 This 1828 image by William Heath, called *A Monster Soup Commonly Called Thames Water*" is part of the Wellcome collection in London.

entitled, *A Monster Soup Commonly Called Thames Water*, wherein a woman is depicted dropping her tea cup in horror after having peered through a magnifying glass at a drop of water revealing its monstrous content. Another printed example of the popular obsession with magnifying glasses and the urban world revealed in its polluted water appeared in the popular illustrated magazine *Punch* in 1850, with the title "The Wonders of a London Water Drop."[1] Here, as in Andersen's tale, the city jungle reflected in a drop of contaminated water from the Thames was a disturbing illustration of the poor state of public sanitation and urban life at mid-century. In Andersen's tale, as in these popular depictions of uncanny drops of water, it is no longer the wild nature outside of human habitation that is to be feared (represented in Nordic folklore, for instance, by trolls). The real topic of fairy tales—which have always dealt with human anxieties about the unfamiliar and unknown—is now concerned with the very heart of the most modern of human experiences: urban life.

Through his many travels, Andersen encountered the attractions and horrors of urban life in the century's largest metropolitan areas such as London, Paris, and Naples, and he would refer to these experiences directly in his tales to instill wonder in his Danish readers in the comparatively provincial capital of Copenhagen. However, the population in Denmark also grew dramatically in the urban areas in the first half of the 19th century. In the 1840s, the movement from the country to the city became a mass migration stimulated by the beginnings of industrialization. Until the 1850s, Copenhagen was still limited to the area behind the old fortifications of ramparts, bastions, and city gates, so the city became rapidly overcrowded by the influx of migrants. The lack of proper sewage systems, the presence of a great number of household animals such as horses used for transportation, and an insufficient and polluted water supply meant that Copenhagen experienced terrible epidemics, such as the cholera epidemic in 1853, a waterborne disease that had already ravaged London in 1831. Such epidemics highlighted the need for proper hygiene and sanitation, and the mortal dangers of life in the overcrowded city. While Andersen's drop of water may appear as a novelty conceived as mere wonder, the epidemic of 1853 would have made the terrifying reality of the overcrowded city depicted in Andersen's tale seem like an eerie premonition. Read from a late-modern eco-critical perspective, Andersen's tale about Copenhagen (or London) may be viewed as a call for observing the relationship

---

1   *Punch* 18 (1850): 188–89. The issue is available at the British Library online at http://www.bl.uk/learning/histcitizen/21cc/publichealth/sources/source14/punch.html

between the environment and modern life, to contemplate through our human capacity for literary interpretation and imagination our own reflection in a drop of water.

"A Drop of Water" was not the only tale in which Andersen dealt with the modern urban experience. Andersen consistently sought to depict urban life in the fairy tale with a complex set of concerns: The city is experienced through the eyes or with the aid of visual technologies; it dramatizes the conflict between the old and the new; city life produces both pleasure and anxiety; and the urban experience is always mediated, not only through visual technologies, but also through storytelling and printed media. While the social reality and technological advances belonging to the city, and more generally, to modernity, can be found throughout Andersen's oeuvre (e.g., in his early novel, "A Journey on Foot" (1829), the futuristic tales "In a Thousand Years' Time" (1852) and "The Great Sea Serpent" (1871)[2], which deal with modern travel and telecommunication), central examples of Andersen's treatment of the urban experience are to be found in later tales such as "Godfather's Picture Book" (1868) and "The Wood Nymph" (1868)—tales that are both driven by a desire for the new and by a sense of loss or nostalgia for simpler times and for the past.

These tales are also deeply engaged in the way modern urbanity is projected through particular narratives or visual-verbal media such as picture books ("Godfather's Picture Book"), newspapers, and a world's fair ("The Wood Nymph"). While Andersen's tales of urbanity may not be straightforward social critiques of urban life (unlike the contemporary novels of Dickens), and while they may be seen to espouse a Romantic view of modernity (Andersen was inspired by H.C. Ørsted's philosophical work *The Spirit in Nature*, which propounded a Romantic view of the path to God through the combined efforts of science and art), they are also tales that offer us a playful collage of modern urban life, which was, and possibly still is, partly ferocious, partly entertaining, and always a good theme for a story.

While Andersen became preoccupied with representing modernity, to his great disappointment, the most influential critic of the late 19th century, Georg Brandes, in his articles about Andersen's authorship first published in the weekly newspaper *Illustreret Tidende* (the Illustrated Times) in 1869, discounted the capacity of the fairy tale to represent modern life. According to Brandes, Andersen's genius lay in his childish "universal spirit," as opposed to the temporary and the merely "fashionable" reflected, according to Brandes, in newspaper articles that "will only fulfill a city for eight days" (356). Andersen particularly criticized Brandes for his failure to mention "The Wood Nymph," wherein, as he wrote in a letter to Brandes, "the poetry of all things material in our time is extracted" (Dal 1990, 216). In 1870, Brandes did finally mention "The Wood Nymph," only to dismiss it completely, explaining, "It will not do to have a fairy tale about a wood nymph separate her from her tree and allow her to make imaginary journeys to Paris, attend a ball at the Mabille etc" (126). The fairy tale was, to Brandes, the antithesis of life in the modern city; since the fairy tale was timeless, modern urbanity appeared fleeting and temporary. However, as Andersen developed his interest in

---

2   See Marianne Stecher's chapter in this volume for an in-depth discussion of "In a Thousand Years' Time" and "The Great Sea Serpent."

Figure 7.2 This 1868 illustration of "Godfather's Picture Book" by Lorenz Frølich includes a view of the Copenhagen skyline.

capturing the modern experience, so too did his tales depart from the classical fairy tale in significant ways, without, however, completely abandoning his trademark storyteller voice.

The most vivid example of Andersen's modern storyteller's voice can be found in "Godfather's Picture Book," which first appeared without illustrations in three installments in *Illustreret Tidende*. The first installment of the three appears in this most urban of publications (every issue featured a panorama of the Copenhagen harbor on its front page), sandwiched between a travel account from Helsinki and a sketch of Paris in the winter. Initially, Andersen conceived the story as a project for the theater. It was to be a folk comedy with scenes from the history of Copenhagen, but instead, Andersen decided to use the popular format of the picture book as a narrative frame and discursive reference. Andersen himself made several such picture books for the children of his friends. They consist of elaborate collages of newspaper clippings, Andersen's own paper cuttings and verses, and illustrations cut from books, picture sheets, and periodicals.[3] Andersen would sometimes prepare the picture books together with the children for whom they were intended, and the images would function as illustrations to accompany conversation and storytelling.

The narrative frame in "Godfather's Picture Book," then, refers to the dialogic and performative nature of storytelling that is central to Andersen's own private picture books:

> Godfather could tell stories; he knew so many and such long ones. He could cut pictures out of newspapers and could draw them himself. A few weeks before Christmas he would take from his desk a new exercise book and on its clean white pages he would paste pictures that he had cut out of the newspapers and from books; and if he had not found the right pictures to illustrate the story he wanted to tell, then he would draw them himself. (Andersen 1983, 903)

The impact of gas lighting, introduced in Copenhagen in 1857, is presented as the historical framework for the tale itself. The transition from an old to a new technology of urban visuality allows the godfather to retell and restore to the collective memory of his readers

---

3   See H. C. Andersen online at the Royal Library in Copenhagen for facsimile editions of "Christines Billedbog" and "Hans Christian Ørsteds Billedbog," http://www.kb.dk/da/nb/tema/hca/index.html; "Astrid Stampes Billedbog" at Odense City Museums, http://hca.museum.odense.dk/billedbog/stampe.asp; and "Billedbog til Jonas Drewsen" at the Library of Congress, http://www.loc.gov/rr/rarebook/coll/114.html

the history of Copenhagen in short, descriptive vignettes, dwelling on discursive portraits of central characters, kings, heroes, scientists, and artists, and the most significant historical events as witnessed by the old oil lamps over the centuries. In the logic of the tale, the old and soon-to-disappear oil lamps represent the storytelling godfather. Like them, he will soon become obsolete, but will leave behind a picture book made out of scraps that have been salvaged from short-lived print publications. As the picture book itself is prone to be circulated as scraps, its pages torn ("Be not afraid if a page you tear, while you look. Other little friends have done it to another book" (903)), the collective memory in and of Copenhagen will need to be continuously assembled and recollected in new material and oral enactments. It is clear that "Godfather's Picture Book" is not a history lesson in any traditional sense, but is instead a playful and very modern exploration of the role of fleeting cultural memories in the creation of a sense of national and urban belonging, as well as the significance of a fragmented mass culture, popular media, and intermediality to a modern urban culture (Stougaard-Nielsen 2013,148).

Though the tale originally appeared without illustrations in its periodical publication, its references to the audio-visual communicative situation, with phrases such as "Now we turn the page," "Now, look at this page," and "Do you see the picture?" force readers to recollect images they might have seen printed in various books, posters, and periodicals—images they themselves could have cut and pasted into the picture books for their children. In this way, Andersen's tale engages the reader in a game of recollection, association, and imagination tied to the medium in which it was first printed.

The urban content and narrative frame were fitting for a publication such as *Illustreret Tidende*—a newspaper that took pride in illustrating and reporting on the history of Copenhagen and other cities around the world, people's everyday lives, and the many innovations and advances that defined the expanding metropolises. *Illustreret Tidende* could not report on the advent of gas lighting in the streets of Copenhagen, as it did not begin publication until two years later, but illustrated periodicals abroad found in the illumination of the city a particularly fascinating topic. Dickens's journal *Household Words*, for instance, carried an article entitled, "The Secrets of the Gas," in 1854, in which the author claims to be able to commune with the gaslights and learn all their secrets.

Figure 7.3 In this 1868 illustration of "Godfather's Picture Book," Lorenz Frølich captures the change to gas lighting.

Gas lighting made a radical improvement to life in the city, not least to security, and it was considered almost magical. While gaslights physically alleviated the darkness of the cramped, dirty, and dangerous streets of Copenhagen, to Andersen they also functioned metaphorically as innovations that could shed light on the city's past, make the city streets and their history visible. Throwing a light source or a bit of magic into a city in Andersen's fairytale world has the effect of rendering the city both readable and uncanny at the same time, much in the same way as the fairytale magnifying glass functioned in "A Drop of Water." The readability of urban life seems always fleeting and deceptive—a book can be torn; newspaper articles and stories, as Brandes also observed, are only temporary and elusive; and the city may eventually be revealed to be nothing but a scrap of paper, a drop of ditch water, or, as we shall see, a wood nymph, who will eventually wither away in the city streets. Andersen's tales of urbanity celebrate the fleeting nature of the urban impressions, technological innovations, and the city as a rich source for storytelling, but at the same time, there is a sense of nostalgia for the past in the tale, for the legends, old storytellers, and oil lamps who have seen so much that will now disappear in the ephemeral pages of weekly newspapers and in an urban present illuminated by gaslights.

This dual nature of the urban as both something to be desired and something that awakens nostalgia is also found in "The Wood Nymph." Andersen wrote the tale as a response to a challenge from a newspaper reporter, who claimed that only Dickens among living authors could turn the modern wonder of the Paris World Exposition of 1867 into a tale. The stock characters and rural setting of the traditional fairy tale are interspersed with descriptions of the many tourists and visitors who daily flock to the "wonder of the world" and guidebook descriptions of the sites to be seen on the exhibition grounds. The result became a strange hybrid of a classical Andersen fairy tale, resembling both the tales "The Little Mermaid" (1837) and "The Fir Tree" (1845) and a travel letter or a journalistic report from the exposition in Paris. The tale's narrator, standing aloof on his balcony in the center of Paris, recounts the wood nymph's life story. The nymph, nestled in the chestnut tree in her rural home, yearns for the great city of Paris, a longing stimulated by the gossip of the birds (like newspapers) and the reflections of the splendid city she finds illustrated in the "picture book" of drifting clouds. An old priest warns her about the corruption of the city, but in a great storm, her pleasant home is obliterated when lightning destroys the old oak tree under which the priest used to tell the children stories from the glorious past of France. The lightning provides a dramatic illumination, not unlike the introduction of gaslights in "Godfather's Picture Book." Consequently, the nymph's longing increases. She is finally granted her wish to go and see the Exposition in Paris by an illuminated figure who foresees that she will be dug up and transported to her new place in the "magical city." The figure also foresees that the nymph will wish to leave the confines of her tree to move around freely like the humans. All her wishes will be granted, but her life span will be reduced to only one day as a result—a motif we recognize from "The Little Mermaid." The worlds of the fairy tale and urban modernity collide when the nymph inside her tree is replanted in the middle of Paris on the square beneath the balcony from which the narrator watches her.

As predicted by the illuminated figure, the nymph soon grows tired of looking at the same houses, advertisements, balconies, and shops from her confined viewpoint in the square. She desires to see the boulevards and the great wonder of the Exposition, and for this she needs to leave her protective shell, accepting in turn that her life will end with the first rays of the morning sun. Her wish granted for the second time, she leaps up like a gazelle; like reflections of light in mirrors, she is thrown from side to side. When she rests for a moment, her appearance takes on the shape and coloring of that particular place. She drifts around the boulevards, visits the Church of the Magdalene, the sewers under Paris, and the magic music garden of the Mabille. Finally, she arrives at the Exposition grounds, where she speaks with curious fish displayed in large aquariums. However, with a new day approaching, her life slowly ebbs away. A hectic fever and mortal fear overcome her, the machine-driven fountain does not of-

"THEY DUG ROUND THE BASE OF THE TREE."

Figure 7.4 This 1893 illustration depicts the wood nymph's tree being dug up to be replanted in Paris.

fer her any relief, and in death, her thoughts return to her childhood home. Her figure dissolves like a soap bubble bursting in a tear falling to the ground. The final tableau of the story shows a withered chestnut flower on the ground trampled on by human feet; the narrator assures us that it all occurred and was experienced "during *our time*, the great, wondrous time of fairy tales" (Andersen 2004, 401).

At first glance, the tale appears to be an urban tragedy. The young, innocent country bumpkin is punished for her desires; she has severed her cultural roots, exposed herself to the crowds and the visual overstimulation of the city, and discovered that even the water in urban fountains is artificial and mechanical. However, while the tableau of the withered and continuously replaced chestnut trees on the square is a warning about the ferocious temporality and unhealthy environment of the city, the tale is also driven by the nymph's (and the narrator's) unquenchable desire for the spectacle of the Exposition, itself a figure for the spectacle of the city. Such tragic desires, Andersen appears to be suggesting, are what belong to the ambiguous fairy tale of modernity.

The link between the fairy tale world of the nymph and "our" desire for the spectacles of modernity is apparent from the tale's very first lines: "We are going to the exposition in Paris.

Now we're there! What speed, what haste, without any kind of sorcery; we traveled by steam, on ships and along railways. *Our time is the time of fairy tales*" (Andersen 204, 381). In fact, by including his readers in the journey (and in the tale) through the use of "we" and "our," Andersen is using an address that was quite common in contemporary newspaper reports from the Exposition (Stougaard-Nielsen 2006, 151). The following description of the urban setting captures the sense of flow, speed, and chaos awaiting visitors to Paris, the nymph, and the reader:

> What changes! What speed! The buildings seemed to shoot up from the earth, more and more of them, closer and closer together. The chimneys rose up like flowerpots, stacked on top of each other and side by side along the rooftops. Enormous inscriptions composed of two feet high, and painted shapes that shone brightly, covered the walls from foundation to cornice [...] The crowds of people swelled, the bustle and commotion grew, carriage followed carriage. There were people on foot and on horseback, and everywhere shop after shop, music, song, shrieks, and conversations. (Andersen 2004, 388)

The nymph and the modern traveler seem to be at ease with the tumult and the crowds. The urban setting does not seem threatening at all as it is narrated through the naïve eyes of the country bumpkin. The houses that shoot up from the earth resemble trees in the forest, and the polluting chimneys are shaped like pleasant flowerpots. Even the advertisements on the walls seem to be pleasantly reminiscent of clouds illuminated by the city lights. The nymph's naïve vision of the potentially threatening urban scenery mirrors the narrator's optimism in the introductory lines, but the reader is soon confronted with the knowledge of the nymph's inevitable demise in the polluted and crowded city. However, as in "A Drop of Water," the figures used to represent the natural world of the nymph and the city world of the Exposition blend in ways that may distort our vision and relativize the urban tragedy.

The nymph is a metonym for the Exposition, and thereby for the urban spectacle itself. The Exposition building is described as "an immense sunflower" on the barren field of Mars, where it will bloom for a short while before it will wither and be blown away. The nymph herself is described as a flower ready to bloom on the square in the center of Paris, and she ends her quest for the Exposition as a withered flower trampled by human feet on the field of Mars. The nymph, when finally set loose from her tree to roam the city, is characterized by the traits of a chameleon or a kaleidoscope. She takes on new appearances and clothing from the sites she visits. She reflects everything, like light being thrown off mirrors in a kaleidoscope. She is literally ephemeral, as revealed when the young man dances with her in the Mabille and holds nothing but thin air in his arms. As such, she reflects the essential nature of the urban experience: the joy, desire, and anxious search for spectacular—yet fleeting—novelties. Therefore, the tragedy of the nymph is prefigured in the inevitable temporality of the spectacle of the Exposition itself. In that sense, our desire for the urban spectacle is comparative to our desire for striking fairy tales; although at first sight very different in nature, the fairy tale and urbanity both expose the anxieties and desires of our time.

The modern experience, as represented in Andersen's tale, is related to the speed of modern means of transportation, ephemeral newspaper reports, and ever-changing visual impressions. Unlike the security of the rural home, the urban space is a transitory space where subjects, turned into window shoppers, only rest for a moment before they move on. The lure of the city becomes the ultimate expression of modernity in "The Wood Nymph." As the social theorist Marshall Berman (1983) reminds us, "To be modern is to find ourselves in an environment that promises adventure, joy, growth, transformation of ourselves and the world—and, at the same time, that threatens to destroy everything we have, everything we know, everything we are" (15). This definition of the contradictory forces inherent in the modern experience is a fitting characterization of the nature of desire in Andersen's tales of the city. The promises of joy, growth and transformation, the loss of community, the urban space, and the stories we may tell about it, as fragmented and threatening, are all present as form and content in Andersen's tales—they are all part of "the fairy tale of our time."

Works Cited

Andersen, H. C. (1983). *Hans Christian Andersen: The Complete Fairy Tales and Stories*, translated by Erik Christian Haugaard. New York: Anchor Books.

Andersen, H. C. (2004). *Fairy Tales*, translated by Tiina Nunnally. London: Penguin Books.

Berman, M. (1983). *All That Is Solid Melts into Air: The Experience of Modernity*. London: Verso.

Brandes, G. (1869). "Andersens Eventyr II," *Illustreret Tidende*, no. 512 (July 18).

Brandes, G. (1899). [1870]. "H. C. Andersen som Æventyrdigter," *Samlede Skrifter*, Vol. II. Copenhagen: Gyldendal.

Dal, E., ed. (1990). *H. C. Andersens Eventyr*, Vol. VI. Copenhagen: Reitzels Forlag.

Sala, G. A. (1854). "The Secrets of the Gas," *Household Words* 9 (March 4): 159.

Stougaard-Nielsen, J. (2006). "The Idle Spectator: Hans Christian Andersen's *Dryaden* (1868), *Illustreret Tidende*, and the World Exposition," *Scandinavian Studies* 78: 129–52.

Stougaard-Nielsen, J. (2013). "The Fairy Tale and the Periodical: Hans Christian Andersen's Scrapbooks," *Book History* 16: 132–54.

Turner, M. (1996). *The Literary Mind*. Oxford, UK: Oxford University Press.

Chapter VIII

Hans Christian Andersen's Tales of Traveling and Love

Nete Schmidt

Hans Christian Andersen loved traveling and was an avid explorer. During his life, he traveled more than most of his contemporaries could ever dream of, making a total of 30 trips around Europe, with Germany and Italy his favorite destinations.[1] He visited a large part of Europe, as well as Tangier, England, Norway, and Sweden. His travels began in 1831 with an inspirational journey to Germany, and he completed his final trip, also to Germany, in 1873, while he was quite ill, and with the help of his usual traveling companion, a younger, male friend. When he was not traveling abroad, he traveled around Denmark as a frequent and popular visitor at various mansions and castles. The view of travel most commonly attributed to Andersen is the poem: "To move, to breathe, to fly, to float, To

---

1 For a complete list of his travels, see: http://hca.museum.odense.dk/rejser/index.aspx

gain all while you give, To roam the roads of lands remote: To travel is to live." When Andersen also declares in a related passage, "I feel myself everywhere at home," his passion for traveling is evident.[2]

Several anecdotes surrounding Andersen's travels illustrate both his love and his fear of travel. One is connected to the rope (exhibited in the Hans Christian Andersen House museum in Odense, Denmark) that he always carried with him when traveling, in the wake of the death of his dear friend, Henriette Wulff, who perished when the steamer *Austria* burned and sank outside New York Harbor in 1858. Andersen was morbidly afraid of getting caught in a hotel room during a fire, so he brought the long rope, tied it to the window, and let it hang outside in readiness for a potential emergency. The best source for this anecdote is found in his diary entry from November 26, 1869, accessible online from the Royal Library in Copenhagen (*Diaries*). Another anecdote relates how he was terrified of having a stroke or some sort of attack, and when discovered, being declared dead and consequently buried alive. Therefore, he also brought a note, which said in his handwriting that he was only apparently dead and should not be buried. He placed this note next to his bed before he went to sleep. The best source for this anecdote is found in the diaries in an entry from August 2, 1875, written by his friend Dorothea Melchior, who was by his side until the very end (*Diaries*). The popularity of these traveling anecdotes is confirmed through the number of retellings, for example, in blogs such as The Literary Traveler. The fear of death remained with him throughout his life but fortunately didn't keep him from traveling far and wide in his search for inspiration.

Andersen wrote about traveling in both fictional and nonfictional genres. His first travelogue, *Shadow Pictures*, from 1831, describes a "Journey to the Harz Mountains, Saxon Switzerland, Etc. Etc., in the Summer of 1831," while A *Poet's Bazaar*, from 1842, describes a "Journey to Greece, Turkey, and up the Danube." His extensive diaries also share detailed and wonderful insights into the joys and hassles of traveling. On one hand, Andersen often focuses on the discomfort, annoying fellow passengers, the lack of decent food and lodging, and the long time spent rattling down gravel roads in horse-drawn carriages. On the other, his joy when describing his destinations is contagious. He reports meeting all kinds of people—artists, thinkers, writers, and nobility—many of them impressive and high-ranking, and he thrives on the recognition he receives and the friendships and correspondences that are the results of his travels. Andersen explores beautiful landscapes, and makes meticulous, skillful drawings of what he sees. The impressions and images absorbed during his travels are, then, incorporated into his tales and translated into comprehensive descriptions of colorful,

---

2 The quote can be found in the first Danish edition from 1855 of *Mit Livs Eventyr* (The Fairy Tale of my Life), under the year 1844. Following a description of the Swedish singer Jenny Lind, Andersen wrote, "I have made the happy discovery by experience, that inasmuch as art and life are more clearly understood by me, so much more sunshine from without has streamed into my soul. What blessings have not compensated me for the former dark days! Repose and certainty have forced themselves into my heart. Such repose can easily unite itself with the changing life of travel; I feel myself everywhere at home, attach myself easily to people, and they give me in return confidence and cordiality" (211). The more poetically phrased quote is not included in the English translation, *The Fairy Tale of my Life, an Autobiography*. New York: Cooper Square Press, 2000.

vibrant, exotic sites, populated with foreign people, attire, and customs, which reflect his fascination with locations outside the limitations of the narrow borders of Denmark. All his senses are engaged when traveling—just as he is asking us, the readers, to use all our senses when reading his tales.

In this chapter, I want to discuss Andersen's enthusiasm for traveling, as it is woven into two tales of love. Throughout his career, Andersen's travels became a significant inspiration for his art, with the above-mentioned inclusion of impressions and imagery into his tales. Andersen was devoted to his art, but his love life was less than satisfying, and it seems obvious to interpret the travel as a poetical rendition of the restless attempt to escape from unpleasant recollections and rejections. To illustrate how these elements are connected, I have chosen to discuss "Ib and Little Christina" (1855) and "Under the Willow Tree" (1852). These tales illustrate a dark and somewhat depressing side of Andersen's view of himself (and others) as a traveler and lover. While we know Andersen used his life as a literary springboard, viewing his tales as mere reflections of his own life will reduce their value and also preclude the social criticism they contain, which grew stronger as his literary powers increased. Andersen wrote about the human condition; existential questions about displacement, estrangement, and finding one's proper place in life—be it through travel, art, or love—are always prominent themes in his work. As the omniscient, intrusive narrator, he garnishes his writing with a running commentary on the events described, often weaving his own experiences from traveling into the message of the tales. Consequently, he relates the tales to his own life and experiences and also makes them easily relatable to the readers, who may not yet have traveled as extensively as he did.

"Ib and Little Christina" (1855)

"Ib and little Christina" sets the stage for the discussion of travel by first giving the reader a clear sense of "home" by means of a quite concise, down-to-earth description of a Danish farm. The countryside is flat, and the River of the Gods runs slowly and majestically through the landscape in the rhythm of the writing. We are in Jutland, in Silkeborg, at the home of Jeppe, the farmer, who "is not rich, but no one in that district would have called him poor" (Andersen 1983, 469). This is a typical instance of Danish understatement, formally known as litotes.[3] Jeppe has a very domesticated livelihood with three sheep, a pig, and two oxen. Furthermore, he carves wooden shoes, which is about as practical and down-to-earth as anybody can be. Andersen's father was a shoemaker, and there are numerous references to shoes and shoemaking in his tales, obviously fueled by his reminiscences. We are also told that the harvest is always meager in this area, but they still have a good life on their small farm. This depiction places us squarely in a Biedermeier setting, where love and passions are not lived out in bold physicality, but rather demurely hidden in the chambers of the mind.

---

3   A figure of speech consisting of an understatement, in which an affirmative is expressed by negating its opposite, as in, *This is no small problem.*

There is no confrontation or controversy in this beginning, and we are lulled into an idyllic atmosphere where one stays close to home, where a shoemaker stays with his last, where moving away is unprecedented, and where traveling is seen as a source of estrangement rather than contentment (Clifford 1998).

The central conflict of this tale revolves around the relationship between the two protagonists: Ib and Christina. Ib is an only child who is good at heart, learns a future trade early on, and wants to give away his first accomplishments, the tiny pair of wooden shoes he whittles, to Christina, who is so beautiful that she "did not look at all like a bargeman's daughter" (Andersen 1983, 469). The wooden shoes confirm Ib's connection to the ground and the homestead, but in Christina, appearance conquers social class. Her loveliness is a gift from God, and the narrator states that "had she clothes to match the loveliness that God had given her, then no one would have guessed that she had been born in a poor cottage on a lonely heath" (469). Eventually, however, this beauty leads to a disruption of her ties with her native soil. Her traveling is not a part of God's plan with her, and in the end, she suffers the consequences of hubris. In the beginning, however, she is as grounded as Ib, with a deceased mother and a father who is a bargeman. She and Ib are playmates, and their adventures are very domestic and tame. They venture "as far as the top of the ridge beyond which was a forest" (470). Unlike the soaring but dangerous Alpine peaks in another of Andersen's tales, "The Ice Maiden," this peaceful Danish setting invites no mountain climbing, no adventure up in the air to find an eagle's nest, and no traveling to explore exotic locations. Instead, they find a snipe's nest on the ground. The snipe is a gentle, wild bird, which symbolically confirms the reference to Ib's solid, grounded life. For them it is, however, exciting, and Andersen paints a picture of perfect domestic bliss that is not disrupted by any desire to travel.

On their first adventure away from home, the children sail on a barge down the River of the Gods with Christina's father. Through their childish inexperience with boats and water, they lose Christina's father's pig, and afraid of being beaten, they decide to walk home, getting lost in the forest. Their first real traveling, then, becomes a traumatic, scary event, but it brings them closer together and cements the bond between them as they comfort each other and manage to sleep. This shared travel brings a premonition of their inner qualities and resources. The fear of the unknown is a major, elemental force in any travel to new places. Historian James Clifford notes that the way a person overcomes this fear and turns it into a positive, personal challenge—rather than a sense of displacement and estrangement—is a strong indication of that person's mettle (Clifford 1998). Consequently, the personalities of Ib and Christina are exemplified through their response to this ordeal, with Ib taking the confident lead, followed by a despondent Christina.

The differences between the two children's personalities and desires are illuminated by their encounter with a strange Gypsy woman in the forest. Andersen taps into the stereotypes of Gypsies, thought to have supernatural, witchlike powers, and he portrays the dark-skinned woman, appearing out of nowhere, as a fortune-teller. The premonition of the children's fate and diverse paths in life is reinforced with the depiction of their reaction to the "wishing nuts" given to them. Christina is greedy and focuses on appearance and external qualities, demanding the nut said to contain a "golden carriage with golden horses" and the one containing "ten necklaces ... and dresses, stockings, and hats," while Ib is content with the little black nut that contains "what is best for you" (Andersen 1983, 472). At the end of their meeting with the Gypsy woman, she says she will show them the way home, but then leads them astray. Andersen says, "one cannot accuse her of trying to steal the children, and she might have acted in good faith" (472), so he's vacillating in trying to speak against the stereotype he is simultaneously adopting. The Gypsy woman is at home in the forest, a creature of movement and stealth, so she disappears the way she came, and then, by chance, the children are rescued and brought back home to safety. They survive their displacement, but it leaves its mark and foreshadows their future path in life. The ever-pragmatic Ib cracks

Figure 8.1 This 1853 drawing by Vilhelm Pedersen depicts Ib and Christina's excitement at traveling down the river by barge.

his wishing nut that contains nothing but worm-eaten dirt. He is not disappointed, but merely accepts his lot in life, showing no greed and no ambitions, content in his grounded, domestic existence.

The next chapter of their life introduces the separation, as Christina travels away from her roots to a life in the city, and Ib becomes the master of his household back in the countryside. As a servant girl, Christina learns the ways of the city, becoming quite bold and talkative and eventually turning into a sophisticated lady, cementing the insurmountable distance between them for quiet, contemplative Ib. Although she has traveled only a short distance in miles, the geographical displacement is insignificant in relation to her spiritual and social displacement. Traveling, then, is described as more than a mere physical movement, as it is accompanied by an estrangement of the mind and spirit—in this case, with calamitous consequences.

Ib had never stopped assuming they would be married, but now he sees his error. When he makes an honest attempt to tell her about his deeply felt love, she merely prevaricates. In his bumpkin-like naïveté, Ib understands them to be nearly engaged, but Christina chooses to rise in society rather than honor her childhood emotions. Her upward social movement, attained by marrying the innkeeper's son, encompasses both geographical remoteness and a rise in status, since he has a job in an office. The high society of Copenhagen embraces a long-standing tradition of looking down, quite literally, on people from "unenlightened" Jutland, so Christina's traveling has given her the outlook of a snob who is no longer in touch with her inner qualities. The childhood scene with the nuts is repeated, in which Ib shows a truly unselfish love in ignoring his own desires so Christina can get her way and follow her ambitious heart. His solid qualities are confirmed, although he also contemplates the dark grave as the appropriate place for him, traveling even further down into the unknown. While he stays true to his native soil and earns a honest living, divine retribution points its accusatory finger at Christina and her husband, who squander the fortune they have acquired rather than earned themselves.

The climax of the story is reached when Ib works his meager field and from it digs the treasure, a golden arm ring. This, then, ultimately symbolizes what is best for him: that which is derived from his native Mother Earth. He has stuck to his last, known his place and his home, and this makes him rich in both money and spirit.[4] At this point in the tale, Ib travels to Copenhagen, encounters Christina's daughter in the poorer quarters of the city, and follows her to her mother to learn the sad story. Christina's husband had committed suicide and left her penniless, so this tale illustrates how Christina suffers because of her hubris. In her attempt to fulfill her ambitions, she has forgotten her roots and has been brought very low, even to the point of losing her second baby to poverty. She traveled and explored, but for the wrong reasons. Her focus was solely on the mundane rewards of external qualities: appearance, status, upward mobility, and money. She didn't realize that her core identity was vested in and defined by the land where she grew up, so the happiness she found was ephemeral.

Figure 8.2 This 1882 illustration by Alfred Walter Bayes depicts Ib at home with Christina's orphaned daughter.

True to the Biedermeier tradition, however, Andersen provides a happy ending for Ib, albeit not for Christina. Ib, the representative of true and unselfish love, goodness of heart, and magnanimity in the face of injustice, is rewarded in the end. The earth to which he belongs helps him, and he is no frivolous fool, squandering his fortune. The tale holds a clear moral, saying that unselfish love pays off, and the reward is golden. Ib is blessed with the gold of Christina's child's golden curls, as well as the gold from the soil, doubling his good fortune, and he is fully deserving of both. Ib is an

---

4 A brief aside about Romanticism is relevant here. The main poem inaugurating Romanticism in Denmark is Adam Oehlenschläger's "*Guldhornene*" ("The Golden Horns"), which depicts the finding of two ancient gold horns in two different fields in Jutland, both priceless treasures from the past (Murray 2004, 821).

artist of life. He knows himself, knows where he belongs, and he finds contentment in this knowledge. While he does venture into the unknown, his exploits function as a confirmation of his solid core qualities that sustain him through hardship. His is a spiritual journey, through which he gains self-knowledge, overcomes his loss, and is richly compensated in the end. Christina, on the other hand, does not possess a similar core and travels for frivolous, self-promoting, and superficial purposes. Her journey is not one of discovery, but of exploitation, and she is punished for her lack of compassion and self-comprehension. Traveling, seen in this perspective, causes Christina's demise, whereas Ib succeeds because he stays home and remains true to his life-sustaining roots.

"Under the Willow Tree" (1852)

The second tale, "Under the Willow Tree," depicts a restless young man obsessed with love, who uses traveling as a means to survive, if not exactly to live; traveling becomes escapism, and it leads to the greatest escape of all—from life into death. We start out in the flat landscape of Køge, outside of Copenhagen, where, from the start, Andersen strikes a nostalgic chord. Although the scenery is not impressive, he comments that, "if it is the place that you call home, you will find something beautiful about it: something that you will long for when, later on in life, you see places that are truly beautiful" (Andersen 1983, 431). This statement introduces the conflict between the urge to travel to get away and the longing for a home, your home, that escalates through the story and leads to its bittersweet end.

As in "Ib and Little Christina," two poor children, Knud and Johanna, are the protagonists of this tale. They live close to each other, see each other frequently, and are filled with warm feelings for each other—friendship, maybe budding love—and they support and stand up for each other. The willow tree in the garden is allowed the freedom to grow wild, and this is where the children play, sharing everything, even the prized gingerbread given to Knud by the baker. The gingerbread man and woman, the symbolic doubles for Knud and Johanna, don't speak of love, and "if you don't do that, nothing will ever come of it" (432). The girl expects the male to take the initiative, in keeping with traditional, bourgeois gender norms. Her love is demure and reserved, whereas the gingerbread man actually wants to eat the gingerbread girl, symbolizing a very passionate, direct form of obsessed love. They dry out, and while the male thinks love would have saved them, the female is satisfied with having had the proximity of the male. This shows a clear dichotomy between spiritual female and physical male love. The baker's interpretation is that "silent love leads to unhappiness" (433); at this point, it appears to be the moral of the tale, an assumption that proves to be wrong. Instead, love takes second place to the theme of escape through traveling.

The first journey undertaken by Knud is a rite of passage moving him from childhood to adulthood with one swift stroke. As in "Ib and Little Christina," confirmation is a seminal turning point, marking the start of new, independent life.[5] At the time the story is set, confirmation meant that youngsters were ready to go to work, with a boy becoming an apprentice and a girl becoming a maid. Therefore, one's parents no longer had to pay for one's upkeep, and in this tale, Knud becomes a shoemaker's apprentice. Here again, we see the beginning of a solidly grounded career with the references to shoes and the adage about a shoemaker sticking to his last.

Johanna's first journey, on the other hand, is a geographical move of considerable distance—at that time—to Copenhagen. As in "Ib and Little Christina," the rural, unassuming Danish countryside is juxtaposed to the sophistication of the capital. Inhabitants of the capital are perceived as being more refined and fashionable than the peasants living off and close to the land. Consequently, moving to Copenhagen equates upward mobility, and it represents the epitome of Johanna's goals and passions. In contrast, Knud has no lofty ambitions, and even though Køge is only about 28 miles away, he is as effectively removed from Johanna's sphere as if he were on the moon. In Copenhagen, the Royal Danish Theater represented the quintessence of culture. Built in 1748 by King Frederick V for the people, it introduced schools for ballet, singing, and acting, as well as the Royal Chapel of Musicians. It was the center in a world closing in on itself after disastrous wars with England and a national bankruptcy in 1813. The philosopher Søren Kierkegaard is reputed to have said, "In Denmark there is only one City and one Theater." The array of brilliant artists in Golden Age Denmark used the theater as their social and artistic focal point, and it was also the focal point of the ambitions of the 14-year-old Hans Christian Andersen when he traveled from his native town of Odense to seek fortune and fame in Copenhagen. No wonder, then, that this is where Johanna is headed.

Johanna becomes a success in Copenhagen by singing in a play. She earns her own money, thus increasing the distance and aggravating the separation between Knud and herself. Although she is taking on the male role of breadwinner, a clear foreshadowing of what lies ahead, Knud keeps dreaming about her and decides not to be silent about his love, like the gingerbread figures. When Knud finally journeys to Copenhagen and visits Johanna, the social and psychological distance between them becomes obvious and very disheartening to him. He literally becomes quite dizzy as he walks up the stairs to the top floor, where the family—aptly—resides, which illustrates how the distance between them has become a social barrier as well as a geographical expanse. Further emphasizing this, within the apartment, Johanna has her own room, pays her own rent, and is an independent person because of her own talents. Knud, on the other hand, has remained with his roots and social class and is forced to wait out his apprenticeship and journeyman years before he can become his own master. Knud is a good, solid person with honorable intentions, but he is the product of a stagnant class model, unable to incorporate social change, and his desires generate and

---

5   In contemporary Denmark, confirmation is still a serious matter. All baptized seventh graders receive preparation from a minister of the Danish State Church for two hours during the school day every week until the spring, when the confirmation ceremony takes place in a church. This is traditionally followed by a family party, and the students get the following Monday off from school.

demand no mobility. Johanna's talents and ambitions shape not only her own social and physical move from the countryside to the capital, but also that of her parents. In that way, she takes on attributes of a predominant male character, determining her own future rather than being content with the traditionally female contemplative passivity of the gingerbread girl. Additionally, her thoughts are not of love, but of her career, which, as the story shows, propels her to heights far outside the reach of Knud's lowly shoemaker's hands.

The break between the two childhood companions is effectuated as Johanna leaves Copenhagen, initiating a bleak, empty, restless existence for Knud. Johanna's destination is the embodiment of fashion: France. Since the 17th century, France—and in particular, Paris—has played an important role as the focal point of high culture and decorative arts; indeed, France was the cultural center of Europe (Beik 2009, 338), making it the ideal place for Johanna to refine and perfect her art. In France, the 19th century brought about conditions ripe for broadening the audience for opera, with the rising bourgeoisie exhibiting a taste of its own for dramatic subjects, while composers, singers, and theater impresarios competed for popular success. Romanticism manifested itself in opera in both France and Italy, so Johanna's desires and ambitions are to become a part of this growing, sophisticated, yet popular culture; whereas Knud's hopes and dreams center on reaching the status of independent shoemaker and settling down humbly with Johanna as his wife. A very distinctive and undeniable abyss has opened between them.

After his apprenticeship, a craftsman becomes a journeyman, which is a particularly appropriate designation in Knud's case. As a journeyman shoemaker, Knud begins his aimless wandering far from home: "He packed his knapsack and set out. He wandered ... without purpose or peace" (432). Since he doesn't want to visit France, he heads to Germany, walking steadily south until he reaches the city of Nuremberg. In this way, Knud places a considerable physical distance between Johanna and himself. One morning, a nameless servant girl gives him a rose in the square. With its symbolism of love, Knud takes it as a good omen, showing the readers that in his heart, he still has hope for a happy ending. Afterward, he enters a cathedral, which reminds him of home and offers momentary peace to his soul, so he decides to stay in Nuremberg. However, his restlessness is rooted in an inability to find inner peace anywhere. When he is reminded of home, nostalgia floods him, but as his reminiscences center on his happy, carefree childhood, it becomes a nostalgia tinged with the knowledge of later events and his aggrieved spirit.

Knud gradually becomes integrated into a new existence, but he is still haunted by his memories from the past. They manifest themselves first in the elderberry branches shading the window of his attic, so he moves further south, only to encounter an old willow tree. His past chains him to a restless existence, and his inner turmoil and anxiety prevent the journey from being a source of *Bildung* (spiritual/cultural education) and serving any refining purpose. Traveling is commonly viewed as facilitating a search for meaning in one's life, but meaning escapes Knud's grasp as he once again escapes from his memories and wanders further south. His traveling brings him no joy, but his concern about the unknown future is dwarfed by his depression, lodged in the known past. Instead of finding himself and his own identity through

Figure 8.3 Caspar David Friedrich's *Wanderer Above a Sea of Fog* (1818)

eye-opening travels, Knud is mired in images of an unattainable goal linked to his remote past life. His feet may cross mountains, but his spirit is unable to cross the psychological barrier between romantic dreams and unembellished reality.

Knud does, however, find solace and balm for his wounds in the mountains and the beautiful scenery he encounters as he walks south. Railroads were first introduced in Denmark in 1847, and they revolutionized travel, making it possible to cross greater distances at greater speeds than ever before possible. Hans Christian Andersen warmly embraced progress and railroads; his international breakthrough coincided with the explosive advances of modern technology in Europe in the 1840s (Andersen 2003, 459); nevertheless, he has chosen to let Knud continue his ramblings on foot. This may be seen as an expression of the propensity for mountain walking that was very popular in the 19th century, portrayed by, among others, the German Romantic painter Caspar David Friedrich (1774-1840). Friedrich's *Wanderer above the Sea of Fog* admirably illustrates the human quest to scale mountains and look at the expanse of the unknown, mysterious, half-hidden world beneath—all in the spirit of Romanticism. Andersen himself enjoyed walking in the mountains, finding the air refreshing and invigorating (as seen, for example, in his diary entry from May 1, 1841) (Andersen 2004), and it seems as if Knud is nearing some sort of redemption as "the sight of the Alps brought tears to his eyes" (Andersen 1983, 433).

It is only when Knud has crossed the Alps and "the mountains were a wall between himself and his memories" (434) that he is able to settle down. Milan is where he decides to stay, for it reminds him of home, "but he no longer thought of it with longing" (434). It seems as if the thought of finding his last resting place in Milan has, finally, afforded him peace of mind. Nonetheless, Milan is not his real home, and he is doomed to sink even further into despair when he attends the opera with his employer and discovers that the featured performer is Johanna, who has risen to the ultimate pinnacle of her art. In Knud's eyes, her singing has transformed her into one of God's angels, and that position places her definitively outside the reach of his down-to-earth soul. Although Knud thought that she smiled at him from the stage, she doesn't even recognize him when she sees him after the opera, and he realizes that their separation is now complete and irreversible.

Knud's fate is sealed, and despite having followed the injunction of the baker not to keep his love silent, he has not achieved his goal of reciprocated love. Once more, his inner demons chase him away from what he thought was home. His obsession with Johanna controls his movements and ruins his life, and he is unable to find rest anywhere. Knud is similar to the mythical wandering Jew, Ahasverus, but it is through no fault of his own that he is doomed to wander; his thoughts are caught in a trap of obsession, preventing him from finding his own path in life and leaving him like a man possessed by the devil. The fact that Johanna is now residing in the same city is enough to drive him away, for as he cannot have her, he must leave and attempt to calm his renewed inner turmoil with the movement of his feet.

Knud's life is controlled by serendipity, chance, and random events that drive him here and there, like a rat in a maze looking for fulfillment, hungry

Figure 8.4 In this 1853 illustration by Vilhelm Pedersen, Johanna is emerging from the theater in Milan, Italy after a triumphant performance.

but never satisfied, never full, always a foreigner. His traveling has only intermittently brought him joy or fulfillment, and when his parents tell him (in a very smug fashion) he doesn't belong anywhere, his alienation is complete, and traveling becomes a symbol of his infinite despair. His parents are homebodies with limited horizons. Knud discards the stereotype of a solid shoemaker, and instead of fixing soles, he wears them down, but he hasn't achieved self-knowledge through his escape from home.

Knud starts walking north, back to Denmark, back to his childhood, but this time, the mountains become harbingers of death. In Andersen's writings, the southern part of Europe, especially Italy, is surrounded by a luster of warmth, color, and life. His descriptions of southern Europe in, for example, *The Improvisatore*, from 1835, and "The Shadow," from 1847, are packed with smells, sounds, and scenery—transporting the reader right into everyday life under the blazing sun. In contrast, going north means returning to the colder, gray, rainy climates with the accompanying cold and discomfort. Life in the south is out in the open, bursting with energy, and in the north it is withdrawn and shriveled. It is toward this shrinking of his dreams that Knud is headed. His heart has frozen throughout his sad and restless journeys, and only the shadow image in his subconscious dreams can thaw him out. His ultimate happiness is reached in his final dream, and life has nothing more to offer him. Thus, he has forfeited real life because of his obsession. His whole frame

Figure 8.5 Vilhelm Pedersen's illustration from 1853 shows Knud asleep against a willow tree, dreaming of home and freezing to death.

has become incapable of encompassing reality, and instead feeds on sad and sick dreams and nostalgia, which will never allow him to become a whole human being. Knud never lets go of his obsession, but carries it with him until he is covered with snow and ice and engulfed in the cold embers of his own passion. It has not been able to bring life and warmth to him, only death. The willow tree is just an image, a shadow, of what his real life is and might have been. Knud is forever a foreigner in a foreign land, and his traveling has been mere escapism. He didn't learn, so his journey, which might have been one of *Bildung*, is futile, and the traveling shoemaker is reduced to a lump of ice. Nature embraces and covers him on his last journey to death, but like the gingerbread couple, he is swallowed—in this case, by snow—before his love has been requited. The traveling shoemaker faces a very unhappy ending.

On an autobiographical note, this story also mirrors an unhappy ending for Andersen's romantic interest in the Swedish singer Jenny Lind (1820–1887). Andersen met Jenny Lind for the first time in 1840, and "The Nightingale" is considered a tribute to her, as she was called the Swedish Nightingale. In 1844, she penned her farewell to his hopes of a romantic relationship: "God bless and protect my brother is the sincere wish of his affectionate sister, Jenny" ("H.C. Andersen" 2011). She was one more woman who was not meant for Andersen, and in the fate of Knud, he depicts the other side of the coin of the enthusiastic traveler. Traveling, then, can also be a path to the death of the soul, as well as a physical death, if one's goals are uncertain, one's hopes are unfulfilled, and one's love is forever unrequited.

For Andersen, traveling was a perpetual path to youth, and he writes enthusiastically in 1866, "Just knowing that I can fly out and away is knowing the path to the 'fountain of youth'" (Andersen 2005, 224). At the same time, he was painfully aware of his approaching middle and old age. The importance of traveling in Andersen's life is clearly illustrated in these two stories, but they are also examples of Andersen's awareness of the duality of human nature. Traveling may illuminate a path to beauty and joy in landscapes and people, yet it may also function as a futile, despairing means to escape from oneself and one's unsuccessful search for happiness—and perpetual youth.

Works Cited

Andersen, H. C. (2004). *Dagbøger*. Copenhagen: Det Kongelige Bibiliotek. http://www2.kb.dk/elib/mss/ hcadag/index.htm

Andersen, H. C. (1983). *The Complete Fairy Tales and Stories*, translated by Erik Christian Haugaard. New York: Anchor Books.

Andersen, J. (2003). *Hans Christian Andersen, en Biografi*. Copenhagen: Gyldendal.

Andersen, J. (2005). *Hans Christian Andersen, a New Life*, translated by Tiina Nunally. New York: Overlook Duckworth.

Beik, W. (2009). *A Social and Cultural History of Early Modern France*. Cambridge, UK: Cambridge University Press.

Clifford, J. (1998) "Notes on Travel and Theory." Inscriptions 5, *Center for Cultural Studies*, Dec. 7. http:// culturalstudies.ucsc.edu/PUBS/Inscriptions/vol_5/clifford.html

"H.C. Andersens Kaerlighedserklaering til Jenny Lind" (2011). *Odense Kommune By og Kulturforvaltningen*, June 15. http://www.odense.dk/presse/pressemeddelelser/pressemeddelelser%202011/hca%20hus%20 erhverver%20kulturklenodie

Murray, C. J., ed. (2004). *Encyclopedia of the Romantic Era, 1760–1850*. Volume 1. London: Fitzroy Dearborn.

Chapter IX

Modernity, Technology, and Tourism

Hans Christian Andersen's Futuristic Tales

Marianne Stecher

"Traveling is living" (in Danish: *At rejse er at leve*), Hans Christian Andersen once said. As an avid 19th-century tourist, Andersen sought inspiration, renewal, and new materials by touring much of Europe, traveling as far as Greece, Turkey (the Black Sea), and northern Africa. Andersen's dedication to traveling is impressive when one considers that many of his journeys were made in horse-drawn coaches or carriages (called "diligences"), steamboats, caravans, even on horseback and on foot; Europe was only beginning to be connected by railway in his day. Travel was an arduous, expensive, risky, time-consuming, and generally uncomfortable undertaking. But as a writer, Andersen thrived on travel and considered it as essential and invigorating as taking a bath: "Travel to me is invigorating, a cleansing of the soul. ... In order to put my impressions on paper I need this refreshing bath which seems to make me both younger and stronger when

I return home" (Andersen 1999, 166). In five poetic travel books published between 1831 and 1866, Andersen describes his fanciful and keen-eyed observations of his extensive journeys.[1]

Today, vacation travel is a rite of modern life. In the 19th century, however, being a tourist, or traveling for leisure and seeking new visual delights and cultural experiences was not the experience of the average citizen. Hans Christian Andersen, famous today for his romantic fairy tales, was in many ways a man of the future, who embraced progress and hailed advances in science and technology. His literary career coincided with Europe's entrance into a new age of industrialization, which included new transportation and communication technologies, as well as the development of the early tourist industry. Transportation and communication technologies rapidly evolved in Europe and America during the 1800s, making it possible for the first time to transport relatively large groups of people from one country to another—even from one continent to another. The invention of the steam engine fueled the Industrial Revolution; by the 1830s, there were steam-powered trains, and the construction of railway lines was underway. Railways would eventually crisscross the European and North American continents, while steamships linked them by crossing the Atlantic Ocean. The revolutionary discovery that electric currents had a magnetic effect had been made in 1820 by a Danish physicist named Hans Christian Ørsted (1777–1851); the discovery of "electromagnetism" quickly led to the invention of the dynamo, which generated power for electric motors, telegraphs, and eventually telephones and electric lights. For H. C. Andersen, the steam train and railway, steamship, telegraph line, and deep-sea transatlantic telegraph cable revolutionized travel, created a new generation of tourists, and inspired his poetic imagination to create a new genre of fairy tales depicting the man-made wonders of the new age.

Examples of fanciful tales that depict how technological advances in communication and mass transportation might transform human life—not least the experience of the traveler— are not limited to Andersen's later works, but can be found interspersed throughout his long literary career. Even in his literary debut, an experimental prose work published in 1829—nearly six years before his first collection of fairy tales—under the title, *A Journey on Foot from Holmen Canal to the Eastern Point of Amager in the year 1828 and 1829*, the narrator is transported three hundred years into the future (he writes of the year 2129!) and imagines air travel and a letter dropped from an airbus!

The scientist H. C. Ørsted and the poet H. C. Andersen had formed a strong friendship which influenced Andersen's thinking and philosophy of life; the two friends were referred to as "*Store Hans Christian*" (Big Hans Christian), the older scientific mentor, and "*Lille Hans Christian*" (Little Hans Christian), the younger poet. It is widely known that it was the physicist Ørsted—rather than any Danish literary critic—who in March 1835 made the famous prediction that, if Andersen's novels would make him famous, "the fairy tales would

---

1   Andersen's five travel books, with dates of English translations in brackets are: *Rambles in the Romantic Regions of the Hartz Mountains, Saxon Switzerland …* (1831) [1848]; *A Poet's Bazaar* (1842) [1846]; *Pictures of Sweden* (1851) [1851]; *In Spain* (1863) [1864]; and *A Visit to Portugal 1866* (1868) [1972].

make him immortal!" (Topsøe-Jensen 1959, 211). The spiritual bond between the scientist and the writer represented the Neoplatonic belief of the Danish Golden Age that poetry and science were both based on a correspondence between the natural laws of existence and human thoughts. H. C. Ørsted's lectures and essays, published in Danish as *Aanden i Naturen* (The Spirit in Nature, 1849–1850), were enthusiastically embraced by Andersen, who aspired to Ørsted's belief that the contemporary writer ought to be endowed with a scientist's truthful and rich perception of the natural world. According to biographer Jens Andersen (2005), "Ørsted envisioned that Andersen's fairy tales would contribute to creating a popular bridge between art and science, between faith and knowledge" (416). Ørsted predicted that 19th-century readers would be increasingly better educated and perceptive, and that literary writers had to keep pace with advances in technology and science, if they were to engage a modern readership.

In this chapter, we will examine Andersen's representation of the new age of technology and travel, in particular tourism as a phenomenon of modernity in four diverse texts: "The Railway" (1842), "The Millennium" (1852), "The Wood Nymph" (1868), and "The Great Sea Serpent" (1871). Each of these texts is driven by Andersen's effort to integrate the "wonders" of technology and modern existence into his literary work. At the same time, most of these texts also express ambivalence toward modernity, as they give voice to the fundamental human predicaments that persist in the modern age.

In a short prose piece titled, "The Railway," originally published in April 1842 as a chapter in the travel book *En Digters Bazar* (A Poet's Bazaar, 1846; also translated as *A Visit to Germany, Italy and Malta 1840–1841*), Andersen praises rail travel as a marvelous invention of modern life—and he celebrates it as a wondrous source of poetic inspiration. In October 1840, Andersen left Copenhagen, embarking on a long journey abroad, finally returning home in July 1841. Starting in Germany, he made his first railway trip on the newly opened railway line (the first on the European continent) between Magdeburg and Leipzig; on this occasion, Andersen traveled over 60 miles in three hours, an experience which filled him with exuberant praise for the speed and comfort of railway travel. In "The Railway," Andersen describes for his readers the convenience and magic of this new form of transportation, "Since many of my readers have never seen a railway" (Andersen 1985, 39). As he stands safely on the station platform, the poet-traveler observes the train tracks: "But outside the station the iron rails cross like magic ribbons, one after another, and it is in fact a magic chain that human wisdom has forged" (40). Andersen's tendency to employ romantic metaphors (such as "a magic chain of human wisdom") in his representations of new industrial technology is characteristic of his futuristic texts. He likens the steam engine locomotive to a "magic horse"—the speed and comfort of the swift ride is a remarkable surprise and delight to the seasoned traveler: "You look out of the window and realize that you are racing away like a horse at the gallop. The speed increases, you appear to be flying, but there is no shaking, no draught, nothing at all unpleasant as you had expected!" (41).

Andersen attempts to counter any prevailing conservative views opposed to the new mode of travel, explaining, "I have heard many say that the coming of the railway would be the end of the poetry and romance of travel. ... I am of the completely opposite opinion" (42). Instead, the author seeks to demonstrate that the new invention and its visual perspectives inspire flights of the imagination—and that a new poetry is born from the experience of the railway traveler. Again, Andersen's choice of metaphors is characteristic, and at the same time reveals an inherent skepticism:

> And what a tremendous effect this invention has on the spirit! One feels so powerful, just like a magician of olden days. We harness the magic horse to our carriage and space disappears. We fly like clouds before the storm, as birds of passage fly. Our wild horse sniffs and snorts, black steam rising from his nostrils. Mephistopheles could not fly more quickly with Faust in his cloak. By natural means we are, in our day, as powerful as in the Middle Ages man thought only the devil could be. With our wisdom we have drawn alongside him—and before he knows it, we have passed him by. (42-43)

Here, already in 1842, Andersen enthusiastically celebrates the magical speed and powerful sensation of the new mode of travel. It is indeed a source of poetic inspiration leading to flights of the imagination. The writer likens himself to a "magician of olden days," who harnesses the power of the devil and sees himself as Faust flying in the cloak of Mephistopheles (as the devil is named in Goethe's *Faust*). While seeking to write about modernity, Andersen utilizes poetic idioms that are characteristically Romantic and belong to the world of the literary fairy tale. His suggestion that "human wisdom" (or "learning") allows us to draw alongside the devil himself—perhaps even pass him up—implies that perhaps this modern-day sorcery might eventually get the better of us.

So, what if we could travel speedily through time into the future? How will the world be transformed by new technologies? How would a tourist travel in a hundred years' time—or in a thousand years' time? Such a futuristic fantasy is the subject matter of Andersen's short fairy tale, "The Millennium" (also translated as "In a Thousand Years' Time"), published in 1852, the very same year as the world's first successful airship (a steam-powered dirigible balloon) flight. It was also the year following Hans Christian Ørsted's death, which affected Andersen deeply. In this prophetic and darkly satirical tale, Andersen depicts naïve American tourists traveling by "airships" to Europe to see the wonders of "an earlier civilization" in "seven days" (428, 430). As in "The Railway," Andersen emphasizes the movement of crowds and the speed of travel: "The airships will be crowded, for it is much faster to fly than to sail" (428). The nameless tourists depicted in the tale are "young citizens of America," who are driven by haste and desire to see "crumbling glories of the past." The reversed temporal and geographical perspectives in the tale are both marvelous and eerie: The reader sees Europe in crumbling ruins from the aerial perspective of hurried and culturally ignorant Americans! The future is now the perspective of the reader; the actual present time of mid-19th-century Europeans is the distant past, over a thousand years ago. One might suggest that in some ways, Andersen's tale, "The Millennium," is a form of science fiction, a genre of fantasy with a basis in scientific fact or in a plausible pseudoscience. Over two decades before Jules Verne published *Around the World in Eighty Days* (1874), a work that gained great popularity among Victorian readers, Andersen had already written a fantasy about transcontinental air travel.

The dichotomous vision in "The Millennium" is striking. Even as the tale celebrates modernity (speed, mobility, comfort, and spectacular visions), it offers an ominous, apocalyptic vision of a rich civilization having fallen to ruins—we encounter Europe after *Ragnarök* (the end of the world in Norse mythology). The Americans who visit the great bastions of culture see only the ruins

Figure 9.1 Illustration by Vilhelm Pedersen for Andersen's futuristic tale "The Millennium" (1852), a satirical fantasy about transcontinental air travel.

and ramparts of past greatness: "Through the air, across the sea to Italy, where the eternal city of Rome once was. It will be gone; the Campagna will be a desert. Only one wall of St. Peter's will still be standing, and there will be doubt as to its authenticity" (429). Like the young tourists of today who visit the ancient ruins of the Incan civilization high in the Andes mountains of Peru, the tourists in Andersen's mid-19th-century science fiction fantasy have little knowledge or understanding of the foregone "European civilizations" that are the basis of modern society. The names and sites are barely recognized by the travelers; Andersen's text directly associates tourism with superficiality: "To Greece, to sleep one night in a luxury hotel on the top of Mount Olympus, so one will be able to say that one has been there" (429). The new civilization is depicted as vacuous and caught in a culture of showmanship: "'There is so much to see in Europe,' the young Americans will say. 'And we have seen it all in a week, just as the famous guidebook promised we could'" (430). The concluding tone in the tale is satirical—there is so much that these future "Americans" will never see or appreciate in the "lost civilization." Andersen's vision is indeed prophetic!

In another, later tale, "The Wood Nymph: A Tale from the 1867 Paris Exposition" (1868), Andersen considers modernity and the phenomenon of the modern-day tourist within the thematic framework of his well-known fairy tales. No tale by Andersen better demonstrates the author's deep ambivalence toward the new age of technology and mass mobility. The setting for the tale represents the quintessence of urban modernity in the 19th century: the World's Fair Exposition in Paris in 1867, which Andersen visited several times in order to write the tale (he was spurred by a comment in a Danish newspaper that only Charles Dickens could write about the Exposition with artistic flair).

The unlikely protagonist of the tale about the Paris Exposition is a dryad, or a wood nymph, a supernatural creature who inhabits a tree; she longs to see the marvelous man-made wonders of the city of Paris far away from her home in a chestnut tree in the French countryside, where "her longing swelled to a wish, became her life's desire" (Andersen 2006, 387). Her wish is eventually fulfilled, and her home is literally uprooted when the tree is dug up to be replanted in a hotel courtyard in Paris, where it will soon wither and perish in the "plant-suffocating city air" (389). Soon the wood nymph springs from the "prison" of the tree, consumed by her longing to see the city. She utters this fatalistic prayer of worldly desire:

Figure 9.2 In this original illustration for Andersen's "The Wood Nymph" (1868), the dryad rises above the tourists of Paris; her life is now only that of a mayfly.

"Take my years of life; give me half the life of a mayfly. Release me from my prison, give me a human life, human happiness for one brief moment, even a single night if that's all I can have, and then punish me only for my bold love of life, my longing for life. Obliterate me, let my husk, this fresh young tree, wither, fall, turn to ash, blow away on the wind." (390)

The wood nymph's obsessive longing and willingness to sacrifice her life and endure suffering in order to partake in "human happiness—even a single night" is strongly reminiscent of Andersen's "The Little Mermaid," published 30 years earlier. In Andersen's most famous tale, the salvation of the mermaid is held out as a possibility. In the conclusion of the tale, the little mermaid does not perish, but is transformed into a sylph, or a "daughter of the air," with the opportunity to earn an immortal soul in three hundred years (although her salvation is dependent on good deeds and the good behavior of children).

In "The Wood Nymph," however, the consequences of longing and desire for another world are ultimately fatal. In this modern rendition of the tale, the dryad's wish to tour the spectacular sites of the World Exposition, the man-made wonders of technology, become associated with a suicidal wish or the "death drive" (in Freudian terminology). If there is any doubt about the fatalism of the dryad's wish, Andersen has underscored it from the start of the story by inserting a subplot regarding "little Marie," a pretty young country girl who is drawn to the sinful city of Paris and falls to a life of prostitution—if we are to understand the wood nymph's naïve observation that Marie returns to visit the countryside, "dressed like a duchess" (383). The old priest has predicted her downfall: "'Don't go to Paris!' … 'You poor child, don't go there. It will be your ruin!'" and the omniscient narrator has directed us to see the parallel fates in the tale: "The wood nymph often thought about her. They both shared the same desire and longing for the great city" (383). In his study of Andersen's life, Jens Andersen points out that Andersen visited brothels in Paris during this period, where he held conversations with prostitutes; hence, the biographer summarizes the plot of the tale as "a story about impoverished young women who sacrifice their bodies and souls on the altar of the big city and are transformed into mayflies" (492). Unlike the little mermaid, the wood nymph is not given a second life—she perishes tragically in the conclusion of the tale, unfulfilled and confused by a strange night in the Paris underground and exhibition halls.

Andersen's representation of the wood nymph's death makes a disturbing allusion to the frequent suicides of late-19th-century literary *femmes fatales*, and suggests that the price paid for spectacular sights and worldly pleasures is far too great: "The wood nymph felt a sense of dread, like the woman who has slit her wrist in the bath and is bleeding, but as she bleeds wishes to go on living" (400). She collapses in front of the altar of the chapel and perishes. All that remains of the wood nymph is a withered, tattered chestnut blossom, and the narrator observes that, "A person's foot soon crushed it into the gravel" (401). The foot that crushes the last remains of the poor creature likely belongs to one of the many tourists visiting the World Exposition. As Jakob Stougaard-Nielsen points out, the wood nymph "reflects the nature of the urban experience: the joy, desire, and anxious search for the spectacular. She also represents the urban experience of transitoriness and loss of home, which her disappearance in the urban machine and crowd inevitably signify" (138–39).

In terms of a study of modernity and tourism, this tale offers more than a simple parable that is easily relatable to the themes in "The Little Mermaid" or "The Fir Tree." In the area of narration, the tale is experimental, and offers complexity that deserves further consideration. In fact, it could be called a "hybrid" text, which blends the fairy tale genre with the journalistic travel report, and as such develops multiple narrative perspectives. The outer frame of the tale's narration is that of the fashionable tourist visiting the Paris Exposition, who, with the reader, stands in the balcony looking down at the chestnut tree in the hotel courtyard: "We're in the center of Paris, in a grand hotel. … Our room is comfortable and the balcony door stands open, facing a large square. Down below dwells springtime" (381). Thus, the narrators of the tale who witness the tragedy of the wood nymph are spectators—spectators who come as tourists to visit the Paris Exposition, but also "spectators" who observe the (soon) withering tree in the hotel courtyard, and thus indirectly the death of the wood nymph.

Andersen opens the tale with the declaration: "We're going to the exposition in Paris. Now we're there! What speed, what haste without any kind of sorcery; we travelled by steam, on ships and along railways. *Our time is the time of fairy tales*" (381; italics in the original). It is obvious that Andersen's references to "speed," "haste," and modern travel signal that this tale will address tourism in the modern age, the wonders of new technology, and thus a new era for fairy tales. As observed by Stougaard-Nielsen, the use of the address "we" and "our" in order to include the reader as a "tourist" vicariously experiencing the Universal Exposition was common in periodicals such as the Danish *Illustreret Tidende* (the Illustrated Times) of the time. In this tale, Andersen has adopted aspects of the reporting style of a journalist in order to convey the idea that modern newspaper journalism lures tourists to the wonders of the Exposition with exaggerated promises: "That's what all the reports said, and who hasn't heard them?" (386). Modern tourists read the reports and are soon longing (like the wood nymph) to see the spectacular wonders of technology, the marvelous man-made "Palais des Machines," a "Wonder of the World" (386). The fact that the crowds of tourists are driven to the goal in a sea of moving transportation currents is emphatically stated in the narrative:

> From early morning until late in the evening they come. Steamship after steamship, packed with people, glides along the Seine. The onslaught of carriages keeps increasing; crowds of people, both afoot and on horseback, swell constantly; the trams and omnibuses are crammed, stuffed, and bedecked with people. All these currents are moving to one goal: The Paris Exposition! (386)

Clearly, the narrator of the tale is fascinated by tourism and the urban metropolis, and by the perpetual state of change, mobility, and anonymity that characterize the metropolis and the Exposition, which is the setting for the tale. Despite the mentions of churches, it is obvious that the city of Paris is a profane location.

The fascination with modernity in Andersen's work is genuine; at the same time, it is clear that the narrator also regrets the dissolution of traditional society. Following the death of the wood nymph at the conclusion of the tale—"The wood nymph had perished, passed on like a cloud, and no one knew where" (401)—the reader is returned to the outer narrative frame of the text of the opening, that of the reader-tourist, with the declaration: "All this happened and was witnessed. We saw it ourselves, during the Exposition in Paris in 1867, during *our time*, the great wondrous time of fairy tales" (401; italics in the original). It leaves the reader to ponder what the tourist has actually witnessed at the Exposition. Has the insatiable longing for spectacular man-made wonders been satisfied? Does the concluding declaration, which mimics the inflated language of newspaper travel reports, demonstrate the shallowness of the tourist's experience? It seems that the wood nymph has indeed perished in oblivion and the crowds have trampled the chestnut flower into the gravel.

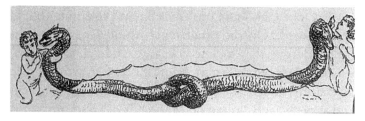

Figure 9.3 Andersen's humorous tale "The Great Sea Serpent," was published in the Danish *Illustrated Times* in 1871, along side Lorenz Frølich's quaint drawing of the undersea telegraph cable which linked Europe to America.

Toward the end of his literary career, Andersen published another modern fairy tale that celebrates advances in technology and tourism: "The Great Sea Serpent," originally published in *Illustreret Tidende* in 1871, was inspired by the successful completion of the transatlantic telegraph cable in 1866. The cable connected Europe and America in a manner never before imaginable; previously, information had to be conveyed by ships (often delayed by storms for weeks). With the telegraphic cable, a message and a response could be transmitted in the same day. Andersen relates the marvelous invention from the humorous perspective of the fish of the undersea world. The sea creatures regard the "electromagnetic" cable as a "great sea serpent," and its sudden appearance gives way to humorous speculation by the fish about its origins and function. From the viewpoint of the fish, the sea serpent is of little use. The old sea cow (a kind of mermaid) is the wisest among the fish, informing the others: "The thing that you are worrying about comes from up there; and everything from above is dead and powerless, once it comes down here. So let it lie, it is only a human invention and of no importance" (Andersen 1983, 1013). The telegraph cable itself offers opportunities for the narrator's wit, such as: "The telegraph cable didn't move; it had its own ideas, which isn't surprising for someone so full of thoughts" (1012).

More than just a light-hearted fable about the undersea world, "The Great Sea Serpent" is yet another effort by Andersen to hail the technological advances of the new age. In the conclusion of the tale, the narrator emphatically praises human ingenuity:

> The great sea serpent of the fable has become fact. It was constructed by human skill, conceived by human intelligence. It stretches from the Eastern Hemisphere to the Western, carrying messages from country to country faster than light travels from the sun down to the earth (...) Human thoughts expressed in all the languages of the world, and yet silent; the snake of knowledge of good and evil. The most wonderful of the wonders of the sea: our time's great sea serpent! (1014)

At the same time, however, there are contradictory narrative voices in Hans Christian Andersen's futuristic tales. On the one hand, he voices an optimistic belief in the progress that accompanied the technological revolution of the 1800s; as an enlightened disciple of

H. C. Ørsted, he sought to envision and celebrate the transformations of the new age in his literary work. On the other hand, these very same texts demonstrate ambivalence toward the modernity they seek to celebrate. Indeed, this is the essence of the modern experience, which is both attractive in its promise of growth, transformation, speed, comfort, and new diversions, and at the same time, threatening in its fragmentation, anonymity, secularism, and superficiality. Johan de Mylius (2004) also hints at this in his assertion that, "Andersen loved technology, the natural sciences, and progress, and yet he did not clearly foresee the consequences of these things that he so enthusiastically hailed. He did not anticipate that in terms of a philosophy of life they would be accompanied by rising materialism and secularism" (35). In a sense, Andersen, the traveler and the man of fashion, anticipated modernity in his works; a study of his "futuristic" texts demonstrates that the author was simultaneously attracted to and repelled by the new age of progress. This deep ambivalence, evident in the conclusion of the tragic story of the wood nymph, characterizes modernity in Andersen's works about "*our time, the great wondrous time of fairy tales!*"

Works Cited

Andersen, H. C. (1985). [1842]. *A Visit to Germany, Italy and Malta 1840–1841* (A Poet's Bazaar, I–II), translated by Grace Thornton. London: Peter Owen.

Andersen, H. C. (1983). *The Complete Fairy Tales and Stories*, translated by Erik Christian Haugaard. New York: Anchor Books.

Andersen, H. C. (2006). *Fairy Tales*, translated by Tiina Nunnally. New York: Penguin Books.

Andersen, H. C. (1999). *Travels*, translated by Anastazia Little. Los Angeles: Green Integer.

Andersen, J. (2005). *Hans Christian Andersen–A New Life*, translated by Tiina Nunnally. New York/London: Overlook Duckworth.

Topsøe-Jensen, H., ed. (1959). *H. C. Andersen og Henriette Wulff. En Brevveksling.* Vol. 1. Odense: Flensted..

De Mylius, J. (2004). "Hans Christian Andersen." In *Danish Writers from the Reformation to Decadence, 1550–1900*, edited by Marianne Stecher-Hansen, vol. 300 in *Dictionary of Literary Biography*, pp. 12–41. Detroit: Gale Group.

Stougaard-Nielsen, J. (2006). "The Idle Spectator: Hans Christian Andersen's *Dryaden* (1868), *Illustreret Tidende*, and the World Exposition," *Scandinavian Studies* 78: 129-52.

hapter X

Gender Constructions in Hans Christian Andersen's Fairy Tales

And Their Adaptations as Television Commercials

Elettra Carbone

The Danish queer studies scholar, Dag Heede, has argued that Hans Christian Andersen's biographical works, novels, and tales stage the constructed nature of gender and sexuality. Although speculation about Andersen's possible homosexuality circulated as early as the 1890s, the Danish research tradition has been mostly silent on the topics of Andersen's own sexuality and his textual gender constructions. This was the issue that Heede's book, *Hjertebrødre* (Bosom Brothers) aimed to address, focusing for the first time on the many references to gender and sexuality in Andersen's letters, diaries, and literary works. Published in 2005, the year of Andersen's 200th birthday celebration, Heede's book triggered a powerful reaction from the Danish media, as well as from the academic world and the general public, due to its attempt to challenge the predominant heteronormative view of Andersen. Although Heede (2005) makes a point of explaining that his book

does not intend to establish Andersen's gender orientation or that of his fictional characters, but rather to offer a reading strategy that demonstrates how gender can be constructed
through discourse (15)–namely "ways of seeing the world" that "almost always pre-exist
individual speakers" and that are much broader than an individual text (Sunderland 2004,
6–7)–*Hjertebrødre* provoked the critics' anger. This resulted, according to Heede, in a consistent attempt to ridicule the argument presented in the publication.[1]

   Although this article will not examine Heede's arguments in detail, the debate in Denmark
over Heede's book raises several important questions related to the textual construction of
gender in Andersen's own texts. As we will see in the texts analyzed in this chapter, Heede's
theories, such as that of the recurrence of triangular relationship patterns (two men and a
woman), do not apply to the whole of Andersen's authorship.[2] They do however problematize
the nature of gender representations in Andersen's texts. How is gender constructed through
words, performed and represented? What is a "gendered discourse," and what are its implications? In this chapter, I will address these questions, while examining how an analysis of gender
constructions in Andersen's fairy tales can offer new readings of these texts and demonstrate
how feminine and masculine are fluid categories constantly feeding into each other. This
fluidity does not necessarily result in misogyny, death of the woman or homosocial or even
romantic relationships between men–as Heede seems to conclude in his book–but can be
observed on the more subtle level of gender performativity. By analyzing two of Andersen's
early fairy tales, "The Princess and the Pea" (1835) and "The Emperor's New Clothes" (1837),[3]
I will examine how Andersen's gender representations challenge traditional gender boundaries and can be better defined with open concepts such as "male femininity' and "female
masculinity" (Halberstam 1998, 28-29). What do these two short, well-known tales have to
tell us about how gender is constructed? In this chapter I will explore how literature can
subvert and reveal norms of gender performativity simply by using clothes and other props.
Using Heede's discussion of media reactions to his own book as a starting point, I will also
reflect on the ways in which these two fairy tales have been recently used by the advertising
industry and consider how their adaptation into commercials can inform our understanding
of how gender is constructed in Andersen's fairy tales.

A Theoretical Framework for Analyzing Gender Constructions

When Dag Heede published *Hjertebrødre* in 2005, his efforts to destabilize heterosexual gender construction s in H. C. Andersen's works provoked strong reactions, both in the press

---

1 In his "Notes on a Scandal" (2008), Heede reports that he was asked to pose half-naked on his bed for an article about
his book.

2 Note that Heede (2005), as he acknowledges in the conclusion of *Hjertebrødre*, has only analyzed a very limited part of
Andersen's works and specifically not the fairy tales (171).

3 "The Princess and the Pea" was published for the first time in 1835 and was part of Andersen's first collection of *Eventyr
fortalte for børn* (Fairy Tales told for Children). "The Emperor's New Clothes," on the other hand, was published in 1837 in
the third volume of the same collection.

and the general public. Heede's outspoken response to these critiques draws attention to the lack of research and critical analysis addressing issues related to the construction of gender when it comes to the works of one of Denmark's national icons:

> We are at war. The reader may not know it, but for the last hundred years Denmark has been a battlefield. Vital national interests are at stake. The most advanced biographical and literary technology has been put to use. The war concerns the sexuality of Hans Christian Andersen.

> As is well known, Denmark already has a queen. That the great national icon should have been one too is a nightmare that has haunted both Andersen scholarship and Danish public opinion for more than a century. Could it be that the famous fairy tales were, also, tales of a famous fairy? (Heede 2007, 155)

Refusing to ignore and trivialize "same-sex, male friendships in both his [Andersen's] biography and his work," Heede offers in his book what he describes as "an undramatic anti-homophobic approach," applying queer theory to Andersen's works (157, 161). *Hjertebrødre* is part of a more comprehensive attempt by Heede to "queer the canon": Before his book on H. C. Andersen, he had already analyzed the works of Karen Blixen in 2001 and Herman Bang in 2003 from a queer perspective, in an attempt to draw attention to gender constructions in their works.

Before proceeding to a gender analysis of two of H. C. Andersen's fairy tales, it may be helpful to define in more detail what is meant by gender constructions and queer theory. First of all, it is worth remembering that Gender Studies does not directly address the state of being "male" or "female," but looks instead at different cultural and social constructions of "femininity" and "masculinity." According to Toril Moi (1985), the concepts of "feminine" and "masculine" are generally used "to represent *social constructs* (patterns of sexuality and behavior imposed by cultural and social norms)" (64). Moi goes on to explain:

> "Femininity" is a cultural construct: one isn't born a woman, one becomes one, as Simone de Beauvoir puts it. Seen in this perspective, patriarchal oppression consists of imposing certain social standards of femininity on all biological women, in order precisely to make us believe that the chosen standards for femininity are natural. (64)

Socially constructed feminine attributes have traditionally been linked in patriarchal societies to all that is considered irrational and sentimental, i.e., emotions and superstition. The stereotyped masculine, on the other hand, stands for all the activities that are seen to represent change, transformation, and modernization (158–59). "Femininity" and "masculinity" are not simply a list of culturally and socially prescriptive norms, but they are linked to what Judith Butler (1990) refers to as "gender performativity"—namely, the way gender roles, as defined by culture and society, are "enacted," not as a "singular act," but as a "repetition and a ritual" (xv).

It is only when we are aware of these gender constructions that we can fully engage in problematizing these categories. In *Hjertebrødre*, Heede takes as his starting point for his analysis of Andersen's works Eve Kosofsky Sedgwick's *Epistemology of the Closet* (1990), in which the idea of closed gender categories is rejected, and gender is defined as "the whole package of physical and cultural distinctions between women and men" (Sedgwick, 29). In this seminal work, she examines the tensions and crossings between "male homosocial desire," that is, companionship, and a discussion about "homosexuality and homophobia" (15). Through analysis of a number of literary works, Sedgwick demonstrates how the division between homosexual and heterosexual has had consequences for the whole of modernity. Attacking those who refuse to problematize and ask questions when it comes to gender constructions, she defines what she calls the homophobic attitude:

> Don't ask. You shouldn't know. It didn't happen; it doesn't make any difference; it didn't mean anything; it doesn't have interpretative consequences. Stop asking just here; stop asking just now; we know in advance the kind of difference that could be made by the invocation of this difference; it makes no difference; it doesn't matter. (53)

This type of homophobic attitude insists on a monolithic view of gender, but Heede argues that queer theory reveals the complexity of gender and sexuality. Queer theory aims at showing the nuances of gender boundaries and proposing new dynamic readings of texts such as Andersen's fairy tales from a gender perspective, while challenging at the same time the romanticization of both Andersen and the nature of male friendship in early-19th-century Europe. Using this approach, Heede (2007) argues that the construction of gender in Andersen's works is, in fact, characterized by pervasive gender confusion, which can be exemplified by a number of recurring themes such as misogyny and the death of women (156–59).

Looking for a *Real* Princess

Although neither misogyny nor dying women feature prominently in the "The Princess and the Pea" and "The Emperor's New Clothes," these two fairy tales are representative of gender constructions that challenge the categories of "feminine" and "masculine." What does it mean to be a "*real* princess?" What is the role of the prince in "The Princess and the Pea?" What does the emperor's nakedness stand for? To what extent is he trying to hide behind his ignorance?

The very first paragraph of "The Princess and the Pea" draws our attention to gender issues: a prince is looking for a princess. This quintessentially heterosexual romantic storyline is, however, complicated by a set of elements that lead us to ask questions about the gender construction of both the prince and the princess. The prince is not looking for just any princess, but a *real* princess. What is meant here by the adjective *real* is not immediately explained, since, as the narrator points out, the prince himself is not quite sure how to recognize a *real* princess: "Every time he met a princess there was always something amiss. ... There were plenty of princesses, but not one of them was quite to his taste. Something was the matter: they just weren't real princesses" (Andersen 1983, 20). The word *real*—which Andersen also uses to characterize the princess in his tale "The Tinderbox"—appears to parallel the concept of "*real* woman," as defined by Moi. The adjective *real* creates a distinction between princesses that meet certain socially defined parameters and others, who could be defined as "deviant," "unfeminine," or "masculine" (Moi 1985, 175). This definition seems to be confirmed at the end of the fairy tale, when the reader finds out that being a *real* princess has something to do with "sensitivity." When the princess declares that she has not been able to sleep due to the presence of something hard under the mattresses, the narrator exclaims: "Only a *real* princess could be so sensitive!" (Andersen 1983, 21).

Contrary to expectations, being a *real* princess has nothing to do with appearance. Although Andersen's protagonist claims to be a *real* princess, the rain and the storm have made her unrecognizable. This is true both on a social level, in that the drenched princess does not have an

Figure 10.1 This 1913 illustration of "The Princess and the Pea" by W. Heath Robinson depicts the prince trying to find a real princess.

appearance that corresponds to her social status, but also in terms of gender norms. There is, in fact, nothing in the fairy tale that identifies her as specifically "female" or "feminine," apart from the episode with the pea. Unlike in other fairy tales, this princess is not even described as beautiful; her appearance is of secondary importance—as long as she behaves like a princess.

Although the prince himself is said "to have traveled around the whole world" in search of a *real* princess, he does not play an active role in the plot of the pea hidden under the mattresses. The prince has no power to judge whether the princess who presents herself at the palace is indeed a *real* princess. The king opens the city gates to her, and the queen devises the plan of the pea in secrecy. Faithful to the gender role assigned to her by society, the queen takes care of verifying the princess's femininity, and thus her suitability as a wife for the prince. Once the true identity of the princess is revealed, the pea—the proof of her femininity and her blue blood—is kept in a museum: As the key element of the secret plan devised by the old queen, the pea becomes a public display, that is, as the narrator warns, as long as "it hasn't been stolen" (22). In her article on metamorphosis in H. C. Andersen's tales, Maria-Sabina Draga-Alexandru (1999) describes "The Princess and the Pea" as a "concise study of the triumph

Figure 10.2 Margaret Tarrant's 1915 illustration of "The Princess and the Pea" shows the princess to be helpless at the thought of the high tower of mattresses.

of essence of appearance, similar in that respect to 'The Ugly Duckling.' In both tales we learn about an essence which is initially concealed, but which does not fail to reveal itself when the right time comes" (105). This essence is, in my view, both a social and a gendered one, which is not visible at first glance.

An Emperor in His Closet

While the gender characterization of the princess in "The Princess and the Pea" is left largely to the reader's imagination and is otherwise alluded to only in connection with her reaction to the pea beneath the mattresses, the depiction of the emperor in "The Emperor's New Clothes" is significantly influenced by his love for—and ultimate lack of—clothes. The reader immediately finds out that the emperor has no interest in traditionally masculine activities like war and soldiers; all he is interested in is buying and showing off "beautiful new clothes," and spending time not in his council chamber but in his clothes closet (Andersen 1983, 77). Outside of the closet, the characters surrounding the emperor in the fairy tale are all men. None of them can see the special cloth that is said to be invisible to anyone who is either stupid or unfit for his office; and yet none of them is able to admit the truth either to the emperor or themselves. In a metamorphosis similar to that undergone by the princess in "The Princess and the Pea," the emperor ultimately, though inadvertently, reveals his true self. The emperor's nakedness could therefore be interpreted as a coming out of the closet, both literally and metaphorically.[4] Interestingly, the emperor's unveiling is encouraged by his male statesmen and counselors, who, despite knowing that they cannot see the garments made by the weavers, encourage the emperor to use the cloth for a new set of clothes to be worn in public: "And they advised him to have clothes cut and sewn, so that he could wear them in the procession at the next great celebration" (79).

Ironically, the dressing of the emperor becomes a performance that leaves the emperor naked, in both a physical and metaphorical sense. His foolishness is exposed, but the

---

4 Please note that the metaphor here is my own and not Andersen's. The expression "coming out of the closet" only came into use in the early 20th century.

emperor still refuses to acknowledge his nakedness, and continues to parade until the procession is over. To admit his nakedness would mean for the emperor not only admitting his stupidity or his inability to fulfill his office—according to the weaver's prophecy—but also to lose his innocence, or at least the appearance of it. It is this lack of awareness of the surrounding world that makes the emperor an innocent child or, as Heede puts it, an immaculate virgin, whose nakedness cannot be sexually charged. As Heede points out, Andersen himself states in his autobiography *Mit Livs Eventyr* (The Fairy Tale of My Life; 1855,) that his innocence was due to a lack of awareness of the world around him: "It sounds strange, but it was so that, in all honesty, I did not think about the world that moved around me, and was such an innocent child that there was not a single impure shadow in my soul" (Andersen 1908, 42).[5]

Yet it is the same innocence that the emperor wants to simulate that gives him away. The truth is exposed by a real child

Figure 10.3 In this 1916 illustration of "The Emperor's New Clothes," Milo Winter chooses to depict the emperor wearing long underwear.

(it is not specified whether it is a boy or a girl), who, unaware of the social taboo linked to nakedness and of the power relationship between the emperor and his subjects, simply declares what s/he sees: "But he doesn't have anything on!" (Andersen 1983, 81). The real voice of innocence gives the emperor's subjects the power to admit to themselves and to the emperor that he has nothing on. Despite knowing that his subjects are right, the emperor insists that the masquerade must continue if he wants to keep his "masculine femininity," his image of refined virgin, unaware of the surrounding world, intact (Heede 2005, 80). Admitting his nakedness would require the emperor to acknowledge his body and possibly his sexuality, as well as to admit that he has been deprived of the clothes performing his social and sexual identity. Without his clothes, he would not be the emperor any more, but simply one of the people, one of the lower classes who, according to Danish author Villy Sørensen,

---

5   My translation. "*Det klinger forunderligt, men saaledes er det, jeg havde i Sandhed ikke Tanke om den Verden, som her rørte sig om mig, og var saa ganske det uskyldige Barn, at der ikke faldt en ureen Skygge i min Sjæl*" (cf. also Heede, 2005: 79).

Figure 10.4 In Harry Clarke's 1916 illustration of "The Emperor's New Clothes," the emperor models a tailored undershirt and smart red boots.

Andersen often associates with libertines and immoral behavior (Heede 2007, 80–81; Sørensen 2004,137–38).

A Very Picky Prince and a Dapper Emperor

The gender constructions present in these two fairy tales have not gone unnoticed by the modern advertising industry, and they often emerge in interesting ways in versions of these stories used for television advertisements. In 2010 and 2011, the British broadcasting company Sky launched a series of TV commercials inspired by fairy tales, including "The Princess and the Pea" and "The Emperor's New Clothes." These advertisements perform, and at the same time, reinterpret—and even subvert—gender roles in a way that speaks to the ambivalent gender constructions already present in the fairy tales, but that is also in contrast with traditional gender performance in advertising, where men use their power and women their presence, their female bodies (Barthel 1998, 8).

That fairy tales are used to sponsor a commercial product is not surprising. Fairy tales, whether originally meant as children's stories or not, can often be read on different levels, attracting a wide-ranging public: Even though they often present unreal, magical worlds, fairy tales deal with real problems and concerns of a universal nature. Most commercials address these problems by portraying a perfect world of desire for the consumer, where any problem can be solved and a happy ending achieved, thanks to the qualities of the product advertised (Zipes 1995, 57). By choosing famous fairy tales, the advertising industry encourages the consumer to create a connection between the message in the story and the qualities of the product being marketed. By making use of the message already present in the text, the advertising industry becomes a coauthor in the constant process of renewing, and at the same time, adapting the story. No matter how artistically adapted, it is worth bearing in mind that the parameters of the commercial fairy tale are dictated by the culture industry (Dégh 1994, 55).

In the two commercials by Sky, the representation of the main characters is exaggerated to the point that they all become caricatures. In this process of caricaturing, the gender constructions already identifiable, but at times only hinted at, in Andersen's original fairy tales are both adopted and adapted. What effect do these constructions have on the story, and how are they exploited by the commercial message of the advertisement?

In the commercial "The Princess and the Pea" the two main characters are referred to as the "picky prince" and the "demanding princess." The picky prince is represented with feminine traits, as he appears to be using his presence and elegant appearance rather than his power and authority to "control" the princess (Barthel 1998, 10–11). As the prince enters the room followed by his advisers, he appears to be elegantly dressed and well groomed. Although the prince seems to be responsible for the plot of the pea in this commercial, he still demonstrates no will of his own, just like in the fairy tale. His advisers, rather than the queen, provide him with the answers, and he lets himself be ordered around by the newly arrived princess, who orders him to sort out his free broadband connection with Sky. The prince's appearance and behavior contrast with those of the assertive and rather masculine princess, who makes demands about her new broadband connection, despite having only spent one night in the palace. Her hair is tousled, and all she is wearing is a shapeless white nightgown. Only at the end does she appear in the kind of elegant, feminine clothes worn by the other women in the advertisement. Like in Andersen's fairy tale, she does not look like a real princess. In this case, however, the princess wins the prince over not by demonstrating her sensitivity, but by making demands. It should also be noted that in the commercial, the pea itself comes to represent not the princess's femininity, royalty, or sensitivity, but rather her ability to speak up and impose her will on the prince. Interpreting the pea as a symbol of the prince's sexual urges, she concludes: "Stop putting vegetables in my bedding. It's perverse!"

The end of the advertisement depicts the prince and princess kissing on their wedding day. The metamorphosis is complete: Despite the ad's playful treatment of male femininity and female masculinity, traditional gender roles are restored—just as the ugly duckling was transformed into a swan—by means of a heteronormative happy ending, with the prince kissing his princess bride. It is this final scene that the commercial wants us to associate with the fairy tale–inspired motto, "Broadband. Happily ever after."

If the slogan of this commercial simply refers to the happy ending of the love story between the prince and the princess, the commercial inspired by "The Emperor's New Clothes" seems to appreciate the emperor's ability to "believe in better"—even though this leads him at times to be cheated, as in the case of the invisible clothes. As the commercial begins, the emperor is immediately labeled as "dapper," but all we see is him wandering around naked. The only items he is wearing are a huge, 18th-century wig and a very small crown that is almost entirely hidden by hair. As the emperor jumps around effeminately, commenting on one of his subjects' hair, he seems completely unaware that he is naked, unlike in Andersen's fairy tale. He is, in fact, surprised by the scandalized reactions of the people he meets: while women simply look away, men run away from him. When the emperor attempts to interrogate his subjects about the cause of their appalled reactions, only one person has the courage to reply: a woman, who, unlike the other women in the commercial, is wearing men's work clothes. Like the outspoken princess in the advertisement inspired by "The Princess and the Pea," she is not afraid of voicing her opinion. Not only does she tell the emperor that his broadband connection is an embarrassment and needs to be changed, but also that he is naked. The masculine woman, ready to tell the truth despite the consequences, is clearly in contrast with the emperor's effeminate male advisers, who are clearly scared of the emperor's reactions. At the end of this commercial, normality is restored by a happy ending that features the emperor twirling around in elegant clothes.

Conclusion

The message of the TV commercials based on Andersen's fairy tales is clear: Women who do not wear traditional feminine clothes (and thereby embrace traditional gender roles and restrictions) can make their voices heard and stand up to effeminate men. Gender is not inborn, but socially constructed, and can be worn just like clothes.

Clothes are, to be sure, an important part of how we immediately perform and perceive gender. For this reason, they are also one of the most effective ways of performing gender in a subversive way, hinting at elements that disturb the gender binary (Sunderland, 188). This is clearly exemplified by the two commercials analyzed in this chapter: We only need to think about the elegant, picky prince and the ragged princess, and of the elegant—but naked—emperor and the woman in masculine clothes.

Clothing is, however, clearly not the only way of constructing gender. As Sunderland explains, when it comes to gender, "the construction of an individual is achieved not in the talk of that individual, but is socially negotiated in interaction and perhaps shaped by associated power considerations" (Sunderland 2004, 177–78). In other words, gender is being constructed, even when there is no apparent evidence of gender in the context of a person's speech. Yet again, this aspect, only hinted at in Andersen's text, is much clearer in the commercials. In the fairy tale, the femininity of the princess in "The Princess and the Pea" is completely dependent on the pea. There is no real interaction in the text between the princess and the prince. The pea is therefore the only element used to prove her class, as well as her gender role. Only a real princess would be unable to sleep due to such a minor discomfort. However, the precarious nature of this proof is hinted at in the end of the fairy tale: The pea can easily be stolen from the museum, and once this tangible proof is gone, all we are left with is the story itself. In the commercial, on the other hand, secondary characters like the queen and the king are disregarded; the gender roles of the characters are defined through their interaction with each other. To a certain extent, the representation of the princess in the advertisement fits in well with other women in Andersen's stories. The princess's complaints about the presence of the pea under the mattress become part of her demanding nature. Rather than a pure, angelic princess, she is portrayed as picky—just like the prince—and self-centered. As shown by the prince's reaction, she is attractive, yet terrifying. The masculine princess dominates over the rather feminine prince and orders him around until traditional gender roles are restored with the final scene of the kiss.

A similar kind of interaction between genders can be found in the commercial based on "The Emperor's New Clothes." While in the fairy tale the emperor's nakedness and his false innocence are exposed by a child—the only one who is able to tell the truth, as he has not yet been subjected to social conditioning—in the commercial, the truth comes from a woman. The gender ambiguity—the child is not given a gendered identity in the fairy tale—is preserved in the commercial thanks to the clothes worn by the woman, who seems to be wearing men's clothes. Her revelations are not due to her innocence, but to her daring nature. The woman's masculine attitude becomes particularly clear when seen in comparison with the behavior and appearance of the effeminate emperor surrounded by even more effeminate valets.

The fluidity of gender categories hinted at in Andersen's fairy tales is exploited and re-interpreted by the commercials. Together, the fairy tales and their respective advertisements demonstrate how our everyday discourses are permeated by gender constructions, and how these constructions can be reinforced or subverted by means of simple interactions and acts of performativity.

Works Cited

Andersen, H.C. (1983). *The Complete Fairy Tales,* translated by Erik Christian Haugaard. New York: Anchor Books.

Andersen, H. C. (1908) [1855]. *Mit Livs Eventyr.* Copenhagen: Gyldendal.

Andersen, J. (2003). *Hans Christian Andersen: En Biografi.* Copenhagen: Gyldendal.

Barthel, D. (1988). *Putting on Appearances: Gender and Advertising.* Philadelphia: Temple University Press.

Butler, J. (1990). *Gender Trouble: Feminism and the Subversion of Identity.* New York: Routledge.

Dégh, L. (1994). *American Folklore and the Mass Media.* Bloomington: Indiana University Press.

Draga-Alexandru, M.-S. (1999). "'Out of a Swan's Egg': Metamorphosis in Hans Christian Andersen's Tales and in *The Fairy Tale of My Life.*" In *Hans Christian Andersen: A Poet in Time,* edited by J. de Mylius et al., pp.101–18. Odense: Odense University Press.

Halberstam, J. (1998). *Female Masculinity.* Durham and London: Duke University Press.

Heede, D. (2005) *Hjertebrødre. Krigen om H. C. Andersens seksualitet.* Odense: University of Southern Denmark Press.

Heede, D. (2008) "Notes on a Scandal: Reflections on Queering a National Icon." *Feminism & Psychology* 18: 410–6.

Heede, D. (2007). "The Dead Woman in the Works of Hans Christian Andersen." *Scandinavica* 46:155–74.

Moi, Toril (1985). *Sexual/Textual Politics: Feminist Literary Theory.* London: Methuen.

Sedgwick, E. K. (1999). *Epistemology of the Closet.* Berkeley: University of California Press.

Sunderland, J. (2004). *Gendered Discourses.* Basingstoke, UK: Palgrave.

Sørensen, V. (2004). *Sørensen om Andersen.* Copenhagen: Gyldendal.

Zipes, J. (1995). *Creative Storytelling: Building Community/Changing Lives.* New York, London: Routledge. "The Princess and the Pea," Sky commercial: http://www.youtube.com/watch?v=9IMlSLhYUzU "The Emperor's New Clothes," Sky commercial: http://www.youtube.com/watch?v=yk5_qaa7i70

Chapter XI

Analyzing Artwork Inspired by Andersen's Tales

Melissa Lucas

Although world-famous for his literary accomplishments, Hans Christian Andersen was also skilled at the visual art known as paper cutting, which employs paper and scissors to create complex images. Just as Andersen was the first to elevate the literary fairy tale to a higher plane of intricacy and meaning (not to mention entertainment), so too his visual works (fig. 1, for example) reflect his unique nature and artistic sophistication. His technique involved an extraordinarily facile grasp of spatial relationships, considering that he worked freehand, without the help of previously sketched guidelines. Instead, he folded the paper a few times, made cuts, unfolded the paper, and revealed a wonderful new world, much as he created marvelous new worlds in his written texts. We use separate terms for different "arts": visual art, writing, performance, culinary, and so on. However, despite the divisions these terms create, artistic works need not confine themselves to just

Figure 11.1 Example of Andersen's Visual Art

one category; often, they draw on multiple genres in order to enhance the viewer's emotional and intellectual connection to the work. This article examines illustrations inspired by Hans Christian Andersen's fairy tales, and discusses ways to assess visual art that springs from, and reflects, literary art.

Such illustrations can expand, enrich, or challenge our own perceptions of a given tale, providing insights into the artist's interpretation of the text. For example, both illustrations in Figure 2, created by Vilhelm Pedersen and Arthur Rackham, respectively, show Gerda, the protagonist of Andersen's fairy tale, "The Snow Queen," in a boat on the river, heading out in search of her playmate, Kay. In the tale, the narrator recounts that "the boat wasn't tied securely, and with her movement, it glided away from land. She noticed this and hurried to get out, but before she could make her way back, the boat was more than two feet from shore, and it began to slip away even faster. Then little Gerda was quite frightened, and started to cry ... " (Andersen 2004, 182). In contrast to Pedersen's quietly composed figure standing in the prow of the boat, Rackham's image expresses Gerda's physical movement and emotional distress. Rackham's version invites us to enter the scene, stand on the riverbank, and empathize with Gerda's helplessness. Pedersen's drawing illustrates that Gerda is going on a journey, but Rackham's helps up to understand it as a dangerous quest.

Over the nearly two centuries since Andersen first began writing fairy tales, his texts have been complemented by many different kinds of illustrations. The first illustrations of Andersen's works were line drawings created by the Danish artist Vilhelm Pedersen (1820–1859), and accompanied a German edition of Andersen's tales published in 1848 by Carl B. Lorch in Leipzig.

Figure 11.2 a, b Scene from The Snow Queen, Vilhelm Pedersen (left), and Arthur Rackham (right)

Shortly thereafter, an illustrated Danish edition, including 125 woodcuts of Pedersen's drawings, appeared from C. A. Reitzel in Copenhagen in late 1849. Since then, myriad artists have translated Andersen's literary tales into the visual realm. We will examine a few of them in this chapter, with an eye to understanding not only *what* they express, but also *how*, which gives insight into *why*. This, in turn, illuminates the artist's interpretation of the literary source. To that end, we will begin by discussing some of the important elements of visual art, and how they relate to the tales that inspired the images.

Line and Texture

One of the most basic forms of visual expression is the **line**. It can be made with anything from a pencil on paper to a stick in the sand, and may embody multiple qualities. A line can be thick, thin, dark, light, straight, curly, etc. These characteristics tend to pair with certain ideas. For example, a thick, dark line may convey boldness or aggressiveness, whereas a thin, light line may appear timid or sensitive.

Pedersen illustrated Andersen's tales using line. Figure 3 shows one of Pedersen's illustrations of Andersen's "The Little Mermaid," which depicts the little mermaid in the water. Compare the lines of the water and the lines of the mermaid's hair. Both are fine, but notice how Pedersen renders the hair with undulating, dark lines, while the water is composed of straight, light lines. The effect of this technique is twofold. First, the darkness of the hair provides a focal point for the eye, a place that draws our attention. Second, the hair appears to move and flow like a river, whereas the water itself is still. It is as if the mermaid is *more* like water than the water itself! This choice is an interesting way to emphasize just how much the mermaid sacrifices when she leaves the sea to walk on dry land.

When lines repeat, **texture** appears. The quality of texture depends on the nature of the repetition. Lines may repeat infrequently or often, be close together or far apart, overlap or never touch, etc. Textures may be decorative, or they may represent, for example, shadows under a tree, folds in a dress, or the roughness of a wall.

Consider this scene from "The Little Mermaid" by Irish artist Harry Clarke (1889–1931), and compare it with Pedersen's earlier, simpler illustration. Note how the use of repeated textures in Clarke's image creates a living, lively world below the surface. Although the mermaid is at the center, the world she floats in also clamors for our attention. Most of the small textures in this work combine to create larger textures, which

Figure 11.3 Vilhelm Pedersen's Little Mermaid

Figure 11.4 Scene from The Little Mermaid, Harry Clarke

Figure 11.5 Scene from The Little Mermaid, Arthur Rackham

can be seen, for example, in the large flower forms in the seabed.

Shape and Movement

Shape also relates to line. The line returns and meets itself where it began. It delineates the space within, and sets it apart from the space outside. Shapes may be abstract, geometric, or representational. They can stand alone or provide texture through repetition.

English artist Arthur Rackham (1867–1939) created numerous works illustrating Andersen's tales; most often, these were paintings, but he also produced silhouettes. The silhouette demonstrates how ideas can be conveyed on the strength of shape alone, as Rackham's rendition of a scene from "The Little Mermaid" shows (Figure 5). Here again, a representation of the little mermaid's undersea world appears. The shapes are reminiscent of Andersen's paper cuttings, but lack the symmetry and connectedness inherent in that technique. Instead, these silhouettes focus the mind on movement. There is little texture, except along the periphery, where details of hair, fin, and rope accentuate the movement. Instead, the position of the arms, the wiggle of the jumping mermaid's tail, the bend of the others' bodies, and the tilt of their heads all conspire to create a dynamic, energetic moment of carefree mermaid sea life.

Lines and textures can also create the illusion of **movement**. To demonstrate this, we'll start with two very simple symbols. Look at these two letters, and decide which seems to move, and which seems stationary: "i" or "x." Most agree that the "x" is more dynamic. It seems to lean, and the curling tips imply movement.

Now look at these two renditions of the protagonist of Andersen's tale "The Tinderbox" by Pedersen and Rackham, respectively (Figures 6 and 7). Notice how the broad shape of the central images creates an "i" (Figure 6) and an "x" (Figure 7). These letters were digitally added to the original pictures to make the point clearer. This means Rackham's drawing is more dynamic. What other elements support this conclusion? First, observe the sword in each picture. The sword in Pedersen's drawing supports the monolithic, upward "i" by paralleling the tree and the soldier's body. The sword in Rackham's drawing, however, runs across the grain of the tree, the soldier's body, the grass, and everything that runs vertically. The result is visually dynamic.

Figure 11.6 Scene from The Tinderbox, Vilhelm Pedersen

Furthermore, the nature of the lines themselves implies more (or less) movement. Compare the grass in Pedersen's illustration (Figure 8) with that of Rackham's (Figure 9). Even at this minute level, the difference in movement is evident. Pedersen's lines are regularly spaced, generally even, uniform in direction, and their quality is soft and light. Even in the case of the fauna on the right, which is less regular than the rest, the general direction of the leaves is the same: lower left to upper right. The Rackham line, however, is quite different. The detail is reminiscent of scribbling, a strongly gestural, dynamic process. Lines are jagged, bent, and circular. The quality is sharp and dark. They seem to quarrel with one another about the correct direction. All of this synthesizes into a strong sense of movement.

Figure 11.7 Scene from The Tinderbox, Arthur Rackham

Figure 11.8 Detail from The Tinderbox, Vilhelm Pedersen

These same elements are at work at the textural level. Look at Pedersen's and Rackham's branches. In Pedersen's drawing (Figure 10), one branch is dominant (darkest, compared to the foliage), and it moves in a generally uniform direction. In Rackham's image (Figure 11), many branches move against and toward one another, overlapping and contradicting each other.

Finally, we can look at the body shapes of the two soldiers. Pedersen's soldier resembles a smooth cylinder, with smaller cylinders comprising his limbs. The contour of Rackham's soldier is more exciting, and his posture unusual. Though his feet and legs face forward, the rest of the body is twisted to face the witch. Such a posture immediately suggests the twisting movement necessary to achieve this position. It is nearly impossible to see such a stance without also imagining the movement.

Such analysis of line, texture, shape, and movement may be intellectually interesting, but to complete the process, we have to ask *why* the artists chose these particular techniques. Some of the differences reflect the prevalent styles of the eras in which they worked, and the personal styles of the artists. Yet Andersen's story, the source of the illustrations, also accounts for many of the artists' choices.

The scene depicted by Pedersen's illustration is the first scene in "The Tinderbox," when the witch seems friendly and generous toward the soldier. The lines, textures, and shapes work harmoniously to evoke a peaceful, quiet scene. The soldier and witch are partners

"I'LL DRAW MY SWORD AND CUT YOUR HEAD OFF!"

Figure 11.9 Detail from The Tinderbox, Arthur Rackham

Figure 11.10 Detail from The Tinderbox, Vilhelm Pedersen

Figure 11.11 Detail from The Tinderbox, Arthur Rackham

when he climbs the tree. The soldier is in the act of moving, yet his movements are far from dynamic. The scene Rackham depicts, on the other hand, is later in the tale and is fraught with energetic conflict between the two characters. When the soldier demands to know why the witch wants the tinderbox she sent him down the tree to find, she replies, "'You've got the money. Now, just give me the tinderbox.' 'Pish posh!' said the soldier. "Tell me right now what you want it for or I'll pull out my sword and chop off your head!'" (7). The artist captures the quickly escalating quarrel by depicting the moment the soldier threatens to draw his sword. Simultaneously, Rackham conveys the heightened dynamics via his line quality, textural choices, and the shape of the soldier's body. Each of the two artists has captured not only the facts of the story in their illustrations, but also the emotional impact described in the respective scenes. This they do primarily through line, texture, and shape, creating different degrees of movement.

Value/Contrast

Another element to consider when analyzing paintings is **value**. This refers to a scale of light and dark. Because this scale is a continuum, it can be divided into any number of values (Figure 12 shows 11 values); however, most artists consider five: light, medium light, medium, medium dark, and dark. The strategic placement of varying values in a painting creates **contrast** (and movement). Contrast is often vital to carrying the message of the painting. To see how value and contrast work, let's look at an illustration of "The Story of a Mother" (Figure 13), by Danish painter Kay Nielsen (1886–1957).

Figure 11.12 Value Scale

Figure 11.13 Scene from The Story of a Mother, Kay Nielsen

Andersen's tale is one of deep emotional pain, grief, and ultimate beauty, as a mother desperately journeys to confront Death and take back her dead child. Nielsen depicts the scene in which the mother meets a thorn bush. In exchange for learning which way Death took her child, the mother must embrace the thorny bush until it pierces her heart. In doing so, her warm blood causes the barren bush to bloom. Nielsen infuses his painting with sorrow, pain, barrenness, and beauty. How does he achieve this?

We've already seen how line can evoke emotion, and certainly the flowing lines of the Mother's dress, and the tangled, jagged lines of the thorn bush reflect a juxtaposition of the softness of the mother's heart with the painful rigidity of the thorns. Yet the mood and atmosphere of the scene are essentially captured by the use of contrasting values. Squint your eyes and look at the picture. Squinting helps to clarify and simplify our view of value. Notice the four main values Nielsen uses: dark (the mother's dress and eyes), medium dark (most of the sky, and the thorn bush), medium light (the sky around the moon), and light (the mother's skin, the snow, the moon, and the blossoms).

Each of these values connects various elements of the painting to each other and to elements of Andersen's story. The black dress, a strong symbol of mourning, is associated with the mother's eyes, emphasizing her grief, her tears, and foreshadowing her later blindness when she relinquishes her eyes to find her child. The white, on the other hand, connects the winter cold, the moon (a "lesser light" in a dark night), and the flowers (symbol of life and hope), with the mother's skin. The association suggests these natural elements are reflections of herself: frozen with grief, suffering shadow and darkness, yet still finding light, and imbued with life-giving hope. The medium values focus attention on the mother. When you squint your eyes, you see that the top left and right corners are dark, but the area around the mother and the moon is lighter. The contrast of the lighter area with the black dress and the darker area with the white flowers focuses the eye on these elements with more urgency and strength than could be achieved if the sky were a uniform value.

Andersen's tale describes the intermingling contrasts wrought by love and grief: pain, cold, warmth, sorrow, hope, death, life. Consider the juxtapositions arising from the underlined words in this single sentence: "But the haw<u>thorn</u> bush shot out <u>fresh</u> <u>green</u> <u>leaves</u>, and flowers appeared on it in the <u>cold</u> <u>winter</u> <u>night</u>, so <u>warm</u> did it feel at the heart of a <u>sorrowful</u> mother" (254). Nielsen transforms these literary appositions into their visual counterparts through careful use of contrasting values.

Space

Nielsen's painting of the last scene in "The Flying Trunk" centers the princess, waiting for her lover to return, in an expanse of nothingness (Figure 14). However, on closer examination, that "nothingness" is represented by highly nuanced value gradations. Why does Nielsen use this technique? Consider how the painting would otherwise look (Figure 15). This (altered) image holds little interest for the viewer, compared with the original. The princess does not seem to gaze into a vast sky, but rather to sit by a wall of sheet rock. Although this work, like most of Nielsen's, is strongly two-dimensional, he nonetheless achieves a sense of expansiveness that suggests the three-dimensional world, through his use of graded values.

Figure 11.14 Scene from The Flying Trunk, Kay Nielsen

Figure 11.15 Scene from The Flying Trunk, digitally altered space

Figure 11.18 Scene from A Little Mermaid, Edmund
Dulac

Figure 11.16 Scene from A Little Mermaid, Arthur
Rackham

Figure 11.17 Scene from A Little Mermaid, Arthur
Rackham

A different sort of space relevant to visual art is termed "positive" or "negative." **Positive space** describes the objects, while **negative space** is what is left over, so to speak. In Figure 16, the mermaids, gazebos, and plants and flowers are clearly the positive space, all of which are black. The white is considered negative space. This arrangement may seem intuitively correct. As children, we are encouraged to draw the objects we see, not the spaces between them, so we are more attuned to this simple equivalency: dark = object; light = background. However, as Rackham demonstrates in another of his works (Figure 17), such a simple expectation can be turned on its head with interesting results. Here again we see the mermaids from Andersen's tale, but this time Rackham reverses the black and white figure/background equation. The mermaids still represent positive space, and the seas negative, despite the change. It should be noted, however, that Rackham plays tricks with negative/positive space even within this single illustration; although the mermaids have been rendered positive-white, the rocks in the foreground are positive-black! The intertwining of black and white negative and positive spaces creates lively visual interest as the artist challenges our preconceived expectations.

Of course, not all paintings include strong positive/negative spaces. The scene that French artist Edmund Dulac (1882–1953) depicts (Figure 18), also from "The Little Mermaid," of-fers no such focus. Value variations do not strongly differentiate the central figures from the waves. Instead, a sense of uniformity emerges, suggesting a nearly unending sea of waves, and underlining the prince's frailty in the face of it.

Negative space is especially important to notice when assessing a work of visual art. It is easy to overlook, yet it often increases interest and/or movement in a piece. Nielsen's painting of the tin soldier and the ballerina in their final moments (Figure 19) captures the tragedy and Romanticism of Andersen's story, "The Steadfast Tin Soldier": " ... she flew like a sylph right into the stove to the tin soldier, burst into flame and was gone" (103). The fire is stylized and oddly organic, resembling the tendrils of vines, while the smoke above forms flower-petal clouds. The positive space, then, creates overtones of life, growth, and a jungle of

Figure 11.19 Scene from The Steadfast Tin Soldier, Kay Nielsen

Figure 11.20 Detail of The Steadfast Tin Soldier, Kay Nielsen

Figure 11.21 Scene from The Wind's Tale of Valdemar Daae and His Daughters, Edmund Dulac

fiery flora. Simultaneously, the shapes formed as negative space suggest tears or drops of blood (Figure 20). With thoughtful rendering of positive and negative space, Nielsen entwines the pathos of love, death, tragedy, and life into a single image.

Color

Now we will look at the effects of color. Color theories are extremely complex, and not every individual sees a given color in exactly the same way. However, artists often select specific color combinations for their paintings such as the primary colors (red, yellow, blue), or the secondary colors (orange, green, violet). These color themes help to create unity within the painting. Reds, oranges, and yellows frequently conjure images of fire and heat. Not surprisingly, these are called "warm" colors. In general, artists use these to create vibrant, exciting, and dynamic moods. On the other hand, blues, greens, and violets tend to have a calming effect. They often contribute a sense of serenity and stillness to the work, and may be associated with water. They are therefore referred to as "cool" colors. Certainly, there are exceptions to these generalizations, but the dichotomy is worth keeping in mind, since such combinations can "heat up" or "cool down" the scene.

Figure 21, by Dulac, illustrates a scene from "The Wind's Tale of Valdemar Daae and His Daughters." This tale seems constantly on the move as the narrator (the Wind) whistles, sings, and flies about

Valdemar's estate. It "blew through the castle gate ... " (316), "whirled the snow into drifts" (315), and "raced over the heath ... soaring and roaring" (312). Dulac's illustration also gives life and dynamic movement to the foreground. Though the weather is cold and the wind blowing, the red-brown-orange palate infuses the scene with life and warmth; the Wind, too, describes Valdemar's daughters with warmth and compassion as they descend into poverty, ignored by their father. The daughters are outside in nature, but their father imprisons himself in his castle, obsessively attempting to create gold. Notice that the castle appears in the background of Dulac's painting. This place, where Valdemar's obsession seethes like the fire and smoke of his alchemy, appears in shades of blue, green, and violet. For all that fiery work in the castle, it is a cold place.

Visual interest increases when "complementary colors" (e.g., blue and orange, red and green, yellow and violet) are placed next to one another. This proximity enriches the colors, or they appear to "vibrate."

Full Analysis

Now let's examine a painting with an eye to all of the aspects discussed above. Here is another work by Harry Clarke (Figure 22). The subject this time is a scene from *The Nightingale*. In Andersen's tale, the Chinese emperor and his palace are described in terms of glamorous, luxurious grandeur: "The Emperor's palace was the most magnificent in the world ... " (133). How does Clarke depict such superlative lushness? To answer this, we'll first look at color, and then move through the other aspects.

Color, Line, and Texture

The most salient colors in this painting are red, yellow, and blue. They are strong—but they are also rich. The orange, billowy curtains seem to "pop" against the blue wall. Not surprisingly, orange is the complement of blue. Furthermore, when a complementary color is added in

Figure 11.22 Scene from The Nightingale, Harry Clarke

smaller doses, richness and complexity result. Look at the subtleties of the blue wall; you will find a plethora of orange.

We find another such example in the emperor's clothing and the objects in the room. Violet accents adorn his yellow gown, from collar to belt to hem. Note that the red carpet bumps against a green pillow and mingles with green jewels. These, too, are complementary colors.

Clarke's line quality is soft and simple, thin and even. He does not wish to draw strong attention to the line (unlike Rackham, in Figure 7), but rather to the color. However, the painter does enhance the opulence of the scene with texture. Look again at the emperor's garment. Not only does Clarke interweave complementary colors, but he also sets a layer of texture on top of that. See how every piece of cloth is fraught with design, repeated patterns, geometric figures, and texture. Even the gems and jewels, the fans and bottles are bedecked with patterns. Only the emperor's face and hands, the rug, and wall are relatively free of textured designs.

Value, Movement, and Contrast

In terms of values, most of this painting is medium. Only the columns on the wall and the hem of the rug under the emperor are dark values. The solidity and spaciousness of the wall, supported by the dark columns, gives the scene a solid geometric framework. The image is not ephemeral or flighty, thanks to their stabilizing presence. In terms of movement, the dark values support a sense of stillness, as if the emperor poses for a photograph. In contrast, the lightest values appear in the lower half of the painting—the emperor's hat, sleeves, face and hands, the cloth under his left arm, the vase with green flowers, the fan on the floor, the tail and headdress of the nightingale. The flow of these light objects, one to the other, creates a sense of circular movement, despite the solid scaffolding on which it occurs.

Shape and Space

Luxury is not the only important subject in this painting. The characters are vital as well. This is, after all, an illustration of a *story*. How does Clarke underscore the importance of the emperor and the nightingale? Clarke's subtle use of shape fastens our eyes on the emperor, and, to a lesser extent, on the nightingale. Imagine the emperor's face is the center of a circle, and ask how many arrow or fan shapes point to his face. The red decoration on his hat, the white-and-gray-patterned blanket below his left arm, the blue pillow directly behind his shoulders, and there are others. Now look at the negative spaces. The red carpet on the left forms a rough triangle pointing to the emperor and tapering upward toward his face. The emperor's hat has two sections to it; the blue wall peeks from between them, forming a triangle that points down toward the emperor's head. All of these arrow and fan shapes work on a subconscious level to rivet our eyes on the main character of the scene. To a lesser extent, the fan shapes in the nightingale's tail and above its head serve the same function. They direct our eyes toward the bird's head. All of these techniques converge to highlight the importance of the characters, and create an overwhelming richness worthy of the "most magnificent" palace in the world.

Illustrators attend closely to the clues found in their literary source works. They transform the written word into the painted image. As we've seen in these examples, Andersen's narrative action ("The Tinderbox"), mood ("The Story of a Mother"), and setting ("The Nightingale") are just a few of the themes Vilhelm Pedersen, Arthur Rackham, Harry Clarke, Kay Nielsen, and Edmund Dulac interpret and literally show us in their illustrations. We have discussed several of the tools they use (e.g., texture, space, color) and how critics refer to these when analyzing such works, but we have only begun to scratch the surface of the wealth of illustrations of Andersen's tales that exist. It is now up to you to apply these same techniques to other visual representations, such as Figures 23 and 24, to enhance your understanding of Andersen's literary tales.

Figure 11.23 Big Claus and Little Claus, Harry Clarke

Figure 11.24 Scene from The Nightingale, Vilhelm Pedersen

Works Cited

Andersen, H. C. (2004). Fairy Tales, translated by Tiina Nunnally. New York: Penguin Books.

Selected Art References

Betti, Claudia, and Teel Sale. (1980). *Drawing: A Contemporary Approach*. New York: Holt, Rinehart and Winston.

Brommer, Gerald F. (2007). *Discovering Art History*. Worcester, MA: Davis Publications.

Le Clair, C. (1991). *Color in Contemporary Painting*. New York: Watson-Guptill Publications.

Webb, Frank. (1994). *Strengthen Your Paintings with Dynamic Composition*. Cincinnati, OH: North Light Books.

Selected Artist References

Andersen, H. C., Diana Frank, Jeffrey Frank, Vilhelm Pedersen, and Lorenz Frølich. (2005). *The Stories of Hans Christian Andersen: A New Translation from the Danish*. Durham: Duke University Press.

Andersen, H. C., and Harry Clarke. (2010). *Fairy Tales by Hans Christian Andersen*. Pook Press.

Andersen, H. C., and Kay R. Nielsen. (1981). *Fairytales*. New York: Metropolitan Museum of Art and Viking Press.

Dulac, Edmund, and Jeff A. Menges. (2004). *Dulac's Fairy Tale Illustrations in Full Color*. Mineola, NY: Dover Publications.

Rackham, Arthur, and Jeff A. Menges. (2002). *Rackham's Fairy Tale Illustrations*. Mineola, NY: Dover Publications.

Chapter XII

Childlike Genius

Reading Hans Christian Andersen through Biopics

Maren Johnson

Who was Hans Christian Andersen? He is well known as the world's most famous author of children's tales, but what kind of person was he? He has been characterized by his biographers both as an ecstatic, creative, poetic genius and a depressive, sexually frustrated narcissist. How do we reconcile these different interpretations, and how do we understand Andersen as a person and an author today? These questions are the central preoccupation of this article, which does not focus on interpretations of Andersen's tales, but rather on interpretations of Andersen himself.

Reading Andersen's tales biographically has long been a popular method of interpreting both his tales and his life. For example, "The Ugly Duckling" is very often interpreted as an autobiographical tale about how Andersen ascended from his humble childhood as a misunderstood outsider to become a famous author. Fairy tales are, however, fiction, and therefore unreliable as definitive sources of information about Andersen's personality, however compelling the parallels might be between his tales and his life experiences. However, since Andersen died in 1875, we cannot talk to people who knew him. He did leave autobiographies, diaries, and letters, but aside from those primary sources, we have to rely on secondhand biographies to inform our understanding of Andersen.

The problem with relying on biographies is the difficulty of determining how accurately the biography depicts Andersen and his personality—how can we actually know what kind of person Hans Christian Andersen was? Answering this question is complicated by the nature of biographies and autobiographies as source material. While biographies and autobiographies claim to present the truth about the biographical subject, they are in fact, hypotheses based on what Stanley Fish calls "cause and effect" relationships, for which authors take factual events about the subject and weave them into a convincing narrative as to why those events took place, and what they mean. As a result, biographies are generally nothing more than an imagined construction of an individual. Biographies of Hans Christian Andersen cannot, therefore—and do not—present the truth about him, but merely hypotheses and conjectures about him and his identity.

The construction of this kind of "biographical identity" has become even more pervasive in the last century with the advent of film, which has become a popular, effective medium for transmitting information over the past 120 years. The box-office success of such films as Steven Spielberg's Oscar-winning *Lincoln* (2012) demonstrates that contemporary audiences enjoy watching historical figures come to life on the big screen. The subgenre associated with depicting historical figures on screen is known as "biopics," and offers a valuable complement to traditional literary biographies. Yet, while literary biographies tend to refer to textual sources for their claims about their subject, biopics have no way of citing their sources. They thus tend to be much less constrained by the facts and much more concerned with establishing an emotional connection between the audience and the biographical subject. In this piece, we will examine how two contemporary biopics construct a strikingly similar biographical identity for Hans Christian Andersen as a childlike genius, and consider how reliable this identity construction might be in terms of understanding Andersen's actual identity.

As we consider how these films interpret Andersen's life, it is important to remember that critical analysis of biopics must include such questions as: How does the film characterize the historical subject? How does that characterization inform our understanding of this person and his or her significance? Mette Hjort (2005) outlines some key issues regarding biopics in her book, *Small Nation, Global Cinema*, where she explains:

> Bio-pics have been discussed in relationship to the violation of "historical truth" and in connection with learning and the transmission of historical knowledge, but they have not been deeply discussed in relation to a host of ethical issues having to do with recognition, individual and collective rights, ownership, and cultural appropriation. Yet we live in a world where culture, more than ever before, is constantly on the move and being transported from one context to another. (196)

In addition to acknowledging the importance of ensuring the accuracy of the verifiable facts of a biographical subject's life in a biopic, Hjort also emphasizes the important connection between the subject and his or her national culture, a dynamic that must be respected in a biopic's construction of the subject's biographical identity. In relationship to our study of Andersen in this piece, Hjort's insights encourage us to inquire into not only how these films depict Andersen's personality, but also how they deal with the question of Andersen's "Danishness" as a factor in his biographical identity.

In order to answer these questions, we will examine two biopics about Hans Christian Andersen: *Hans Christian Andersen: My Life as a Fairytale* (2003), which was produced by the American company Hallmark Entertainment, and *Unge Andersen* (Young Andersen) (2005), which was produced by three Scandinavian production companies. My analysis will focus on how these two films, produced during the same time period in different national contexts, characterize Andersen as an individual and as a national symbol. While both films construct a similar image of Andersen as childlike, naïve, ignorant, and a careless genius, they differ considerably in their depiction of Andersen in relation to two national contexts.

Andersen's Biographical Identity: The Childlike Genius

The image of Andersen as a childlike genius that appears in both biopics derives originally from an essay about Andersen that was written by the Danish literary critic, Georg Brandes. Brandes was a prolific and influential literary critic in 19th-century Europe, whose commentaries on culture and literature had a profound impact in that century. In his essay, "*H. C. Andersen som Æventyrdigter*" (H. C. Andersen as a Fairy-Tale Poet), published in 1869, six years before Andersen's death, Brandes tries to identify how Andersen achieved such success as an author of children's tales. He equates Andersen's "genius," or unique skills that distinguish him from his peers, with his ability to write tales that appeal to the sensibilities of children:

> Just like the familiar figures of children in antique times, his infantile "genius" plays with masks, evokes laughter, amuses, and intimidates from behind them. In this way the fairy tale in all its straightforwardness, masked expression becomes his voice's natural, even classical tone, that rarely goes too far or sounds inauthentic. (Brandes 1984, 96)[1]

For Brandes, Andersen's genius lies in his ability to adapt his narrative style to appeal to children. Brandes does not claim that Andersen is a child, of course, but rather that Andersen is able to use masks to disguise his adult identity when writing tales for children.

---

1 "*Hans barnlige Genius leger som de bekendte antike Børneskikkelser med Masken, vækker Latter, morer og skræmmer bag den. Saaledes bliver Æventyrets i al sin Ligefremed maskerede Udtryksmaade hans Stemmes naturlige, ja klassiske Tonefald, der meget sjældent slaar over eller klinger falsk.*" My translation.

Although nearly a century and a half has passed since the publication of Brandes's article, his attribution of Andersen's genius to his childlike nature continues to be normative for popular views of Andersen, as our analysis of the two biopics on Andersen produced around the 200th anniversary of his birth in 2005, will reveal.

Before we turn to those films, however, it may be helpful to learn that these recent films are not the first biopics to be made about Hans Christian Andersen. Already in 1939, the famous Danish director Carl Dreyer (1889–1968) wrote an article titled, "New Roads for the Danish Film—Hans Christian Andersen," in which he outlines the parameters for an acceptably authentic cinematic biography of Denmark's most famous author. Hjort (2005) explains that Dreyer believes that the "constitutive norms and pragmatic end of the bio-pic genre ... should be predicated on the idea of personhood and its faithful articulation, with the ultimate aim of transforming individual achievement into a symbol of the nation within a larger politics of recognition" (197). Dreyer's first requirement is that the film must provide a "faithful" representation of the subject, meaning that a biopic must present a biographical identity that is grounded in facts, which would be validated by public affirmation of the cinematic depiction: "Indeed, in his mind, the Danish nation's public endorsement of a Hans Christian Andersen bio-pic would count as proof that the norm of an authentic representation of personhood has been met" (197). A given biopic could only be considered an acceptable and valid representation of a national star like Hans Christian Andersen if it receives the endorsement of the Danish public, much as the American people endorsed Spielberg's representation of Abraham "Lincoln."

Dreyer's second requirement deals with the relationship between the biopic and the nation that the individual represents. In Dreyer's view, biopics are capable of attaining international importance due of the global nature of the film industry, with the result that a biographical subject can thereby function as a symbol of a particular nation's greatness. For these reasons, Dreyer believed that a Danish production company ought to produce an Andersen biopic, in order to ensure a construction of Andersen's biographical identity that was both factually and culturally correct. He feared that a Hollywood manipulation of Andersen's biography would minimize his cultural significance as a Dane, as Hjort explains: "Danes, in short, are encouraged to assert their right to their cultural heritage by making the bio-pic themselves and by ignoring Hollywood norms that would favor fictitious love plots and sex appeal" (198). Dreyer goes so far as to say that it is the right of the Danish film industry to produce a biopic on Andersen because Andersen is an important part of Danish culture and heritage. Production of an Andersen biopic in Denmark, in Dreyer's eyes, would ensure Andersen's place as a representative of Danish greatness throughout the world.

Dreyer's calls were not heeded by the Danish film industry; instead, the Hungarian director Charles Vidor produced the first biopic, *Hans Christian Andersen*, for Samuel Goldwyn Productions in Hollywood in 1952, with the charismatic Danny Kaye in the title role. Vidor's film, a musical that portrays Andersen as lovable, naïve, and creative, is significant both in terms of its representation of Andersen and its involvement with the larger question of cultural ownership of national icons. The film opens with Andersen surrounded by children in the early morning reciting his tales. Andersen enthralls the children, and even as the school bell rings in the background, they attentively listen to the tales. In this film, Andersen is presented as an engaging, charismatic storyteller and irrepressible singer. Indeed, the cheerful, vivacious image of Andersen embodied by Kaye has been highly influential in shaping public perception of the author ever since. Kaye was even knighted by Denmark's queen Margrethe II in 1983 for his performance. By producing his film in Hollywood, however, Vidor implicitly challenged Danish control of the narrative of Andersen's biographical identity—in film, at least. The debate about who "owns" Andersen on screen was not revived until more than half a century later with the production of the two films that we'll examine in this chapter.

Figure 12.1 Danny Kaye's depiction of Hans Christian Andersen in RKO's film had global influence on popular perceptions of Andersen's personality.

Hans Christian Andersen: My Life as a Fairytale (2003)

The first movie we'll analyze, *Hans Christian Andersen: My Life as a Fairytale*, made by Hallmark in 2003, takes its title from Andersen's autobiography, *Mit Livs Eventyr* (The Fairy Tale of My Life; 1855). The jacket for the film reads, "His world was magical. His legacy ... immortal." Rather than providing any cultural specificity, this blurb foregrounds the immaturity and universality of Andersen's works. A Hallmark Home Entertainment production, the film was distributed primarily in the United States. The film stars Kieran Bew as Hans Christian Andersen and James Fox as Jonas Collin, Andersen's benefactor. The film weaves Andersen's biography and tales together and seems to attribute many of Andersen's tales to his own life experiences.

Hans Christian Andersen: My Life as a Fairytale begins with a close-up shot of an energetic, yet juvenile, adolescent young man whom we soon identify as Hans Christian Andersen. The film begins in Andersen's hometown of Odense, Denmark, where his mother works as a laundress and his father, a former soldier, is shown to be severely ill, and therefore unable to work. The filmmakers use a monotone color palette in the first scenes of the film to portray the poverty of the Andersen family. Hans Christian Andersen is introduced in the film as an adolescent, possibly 13 or 14 years old. In 19th-century Denmark, early adolescence would be the time when a young man would start contributing to his family's economy, but in the film, although Andersen appears to be the size of a grown-up, his behavior is far from adult. He runs around the village, distracting his mother and making up stories with small wooden figurines. Even though everyone in the village seems to have a job or a chore to complete, Hans Christian lives blissfully in the world of his imagination, unaware of the practical responsibilities of real life. The one time Andersen recognizes the world around him is when circus performers arrive in Odense and perform on the main street of town. Andersen is drawn to them and tries to perform with them. Unfortunately Andersen's enthusiasm for the circus is mocked by the circus performers and fellow observers; a young man of Andersen's stature and age should not be interested in circus performers—he should be working and earning money. Andersen's childlike behavior clashes with social norms regarding adolescent boys at that time. Instead of helping his mother and assuming responsibilities associated with being an adult, like being helpful or even trying to earn money for his poor family, Andersen is shown to be preoccupied by the world of the imagination, like a young child.

Although the film shows that Andersen's mother is frustrated by his inability to assume responsibility for earning money and his continued fascination with the world of stories, it also establishes his potential for greatness. When Andersen's mother sends him to do his chores, he gets distracted by one of his mother's friends, who is a palm reader. He pleads with her to tell his fortune and, with great amazement and enthusiasm, she reveals: "It says, one day, Hans, that the whole of Copenhagen will be lit up in your honor—in your honor." Her eyes are filled with energy and excitement as she relates her reading of Andersen's fate. Unlike Andersen's mother, she believes that Andersen's stories may make him famous one day. The palm reading merely reinforces Andersen's uniqueness and special talents for Andersen and for the viewers of the film. Is it his childlike behavior, his unquenchable curiosity that makes him special?

These opening scenes of the film present an interpretation of Andersen that is reminiscent of Brandes's assessment of Andersen's genius as a function of his immaturity. In this scene, Andersen appears as naïve, innocent, caught in his world of fantasy. Andersen's own reaction to this encouraging prediction mirrors the expression on the fortune-teller's face. His face shows excitement, delight, and amazement at the possibility of such good fortune. He displays childlike energy. His excitement is pure—it is not clouded by fear of failure or inadequacy. He does not display any of the doubts or skepticism typical of an adult, but believes wholeheartedly in his destiny. The film reinforces the viewer's perception of Andersen's impetuosity by depicting his apparently spontaneous decision to travel immediately to Copenhagen, penniless and alone, to follow his dream of becoming famous.

Given his humble beginnings in Odense, Andersen's ambitions seem ridiculous, even more so because of his naïveté toward the world. When Andersen arrives in Copenhagen, he finds himself in the midst of the largest city in Denmark, with no relations and hardly any money. The film dwells on his bewilderment and awkwardness, making it obvious that he has no plan for how to make the connections or pursue the opportunities necessary to introduce himself to the artistic circles of Copenhagen. Instead, he acts like an unruly child, trying to draw attention to himself. He shows up at theater performances and concerts, barging in without a ticket or even any apparent recognition that he needs a ticket. His desire to be a star overshadows any awareness he may have of social norms, making him appear a fool. People around him are shown to marvel at how a young man could be so blind to ordinary social sensibilities. During a meeting of important theater officials in Copenhagen, Andersen bursts in and demands an audition as an actor. He hops right on to the conference table and begins to perform a piece from a play he has written (Figure 2). His presence is clearly unwelcome, and the positioning of Andersen on the table in

Figure 12.2 This still from the Hallmark film *Hans Christian Andersen: My Life as a Fairytale (2003)* underscores the immaturity of Andersen's character.

juxtaposition to the men who are considered "cultural elites" makes him look juvenile and ill-bred. The inappropriateness of Andersen's behavior is confirmed by the reaction of one of the men in the meeting, whose facial expression reflects disbelief that someone who appears to be a young adult would behave in such a way. By his behavior, Andersen does not present himself as an adult would, and as a result, creates tension between the adult-child and the adult men—who, the viewer assumes, are suspicious of Andersen and must be leery of encouraging him in his ambitions.

Despite this outrageous behavior, or perhaps precisely because of it, Andersen finds a mentor among the theater administrators, Jonas Collin, and gets the financial support he needs to launch his career as a writer. Andersen's writing career becomes the focus of the rest of the film. Several of his tales, like "The Snow Queen" and "The Little Mermaid," are reenacted and woven into the film's presentation of Andersen's biography. Although Andersen's childish antics ought to place him at a disadvantage in a society as concerned with manners and social class as early-19th-century Denmark, his youthful enthusiasm and nascent poetic abilities set him apart from others, allowing a discerning adult like Collin to recognize the imaginative artistic potential hidden behind, and possibly even nourished by, Andersen's immature behavior.

These two scenes in the movie are examples of how the film constructs Andersen's biographical identity as a childlike genius, without any particular emphasis on his Danish national identity. Whether out of ignorance or indifference, the film makes little effort to explore the Danish sociohistorical or physical context of Andersen's youth, education, or early career, focusing instead on the author's idiosyncratic rise to fame and on particular events that may have inspired the composition of his fairy tales, most of which are set in enclosed spaces that lack cultural or historical specificity. The film fails to explore the maturation of Andersen's character as he ages, with the result that his naive curiosity and juvenile excitement about the world remain his dominant character traits. The outcome of this one-dimensional depiction of the famous storyteller is to construct an image of him as frozen in time, an overgrown child living in a fantasy world of his own invention that finds expression in his fairy tales.

Unge Andersen (2005)

The second film we'll examine, *Unge Andersen* (Young Andersen; 2005), was produced by Nordisk Film, Sverige Television, and Norsk Rikskringkasting, a trilateral production team between film and television industries in Denmark, Sweden, and Norway. Its release in 2005 coincided with the bicentennial celebration of Andersen's birth, which was the occasion for national and international celebrations of Andersen, his tales, and his legacy. The festivities in Denmark were an important affirmation of Andersen's continued significance to contemporary Danish culture. The film, which stars Simon Dahl Thaulow as the adolescent Andersen, Peter Steen as the elderly H. C. Andersen, and Henning Jensen as Andersen's tutor, Rector Meisling, received financial support from the H. C. Andersen budget for the 2005 celebrations. The film is narrated by an elderly, sickly Andersen, who is looking back on his life, remembering the unhappy days of his education under the strict tutelage of Rector Meisling. As in the Hallmark film, this film's depiction of Andersen's genius as a product of his childlike nature echoes Brandes's characterization of him. However, the image of Andersen as childlike is employed differently in this film. In particular, the presence of the elderly Andersen in the narrative frame reminds viewers that although the film is about the trials of an adolescent boy, he does eventually grow up into a world-famous author and respected member of Denmark's cultural elite.

Figure 12.3 This still from the film *Unge Andersen (2005)* shows Andersen being confronted by his hostile teacher, Simon Meisling.

Although the film does depict several incidents from Andersen's childhood and his initial attempts to find a mentor in Copenhagen, it concentrates primarily on Andersen's struggle to obtain a formal education without stifling his talent. In 1822, Andersen's benefactor, Jonas Collin, one of the directors of the Royal Danish Theater, sent Andersen to the home of a teacher named Simon Meisling in Slagelse to live with him and attend his school. Based on Andersen's autobiography and other sources, it seems that time at Meisling's school was one of the darkest periods of his life, but also one of the most formative for his later career. Meisling was likely either threatened or intimidated by Andersen, and therefore was not interested in helping Andersen cultivate his literary creativity, which is the main source of tension in the film. In the film, dark skies and rain greet Andersen upon his arrival in Meisling's village, foreshadowing the stormy relationship between teacher and pupil. Andersen steps out of the carriage in Slagelse and is greeted by Meisling with the terse remark: "Sent here by a counselor of state. You must be a genius." (Figure 3) The line is spoken with great sarcasm and contempt. It is clear that Meisling is not interested in Andersen's potential as a student; instead, he wants to establish his authority over Andersen. Furthermore, Meisling is suspicious of why a benefactor like Jonas Collin would be so interested in an adolescent boy like Andersen who has so little formal education—what could be so special about this young man?

The relationship between Meisling and Andersen is shown to resemble that of an overbearing father and a rebellious son, which serves to reinforce Andersen's childlike persona. Meisling does not want to encourage Andersen's creativity, and seeks to squash his imagination. He wants Andersen to obey all of his rules, both at home and at school. He perceives Andersen's creativity as a threat to the order of his school and his patriarchal power. He bans Andersen from writing, and orders him to only focus on his schoolwork as a way to control his creative impulses. Meisling describes Andersen's imagination as "dangerous," and he seems to see it as threatening to his position of power in the school. Meisling's strict disciplinary measures with Andersen are his way of positioning Andersen as his subordinate. Meisling did not respect Andersen, and saw his presence only as a way to benefit financially and gain the favor of powerful men like Jonas Collin. Andersen responds to this harsh treatment with tears, tantrums, and a retreat into his fanciful friendship with another young boy, called "Little Tuk."

In contrast to the Hallmark film, which focuses exclusively on Andersen's naive and juvenile personality, the Nordisk biopic presents a much more complex characterization of Andersen. Although it makes use of Brandes's characterization of the childlike quality of Andersen's poetic genius, the film also makes it clear, in particular through the strategy of framing the depiction of the adolescent Andersen by scenes featuring the elderly, sickly Andersen, that the author's naive, childlike traits belong to a particular phase in the author's development. This phase is, arguably, key to Andersen's genius and success, but which cannot encompass the entirety of his life experiences or the complexity of his personality. Rather than assuming a static personality, *Unge Andersen* allows for the development of Andersen's character, both as he grows from an awkward adolescent into a man, and from a fledgling poet into a confident author.

Another significant difference between the two biopics is the extent to which Andersen's Danish identity is present in the film. While neither film makes "Danishness" a central concern, the meticulous depiction of early-19th-century Denmark in *Unge Andersen*, from the unpaved streets of Slagelse to the impressive facade of the Royal Theater to the brothels of the back streets of the walled city of Copenhagen, gives the film credibility as a historical source and foregrounds the sociocultural conditions of Andersen's formative years.

Moreover, the Nordisk film's decision to avoid excessive biographical associations between Andersen's life and works, in order to focus more closely on the process of inspiration and composition, establishes Andersen's genius as more than simply a spontaneous function of his (peculiar) personality. Instead, it is a talent fostered by the mentoring of such men as Jonas Collin, the king of Denmark, and even Simon Meisling, as well as Andersen's dear friend, Henriette Wulff, all of whom figure prominently in Danish society of the time. As the saying goes, it takes a village to raise a child; this film makes it clear that Andersen's rise to fame was facilitated by members of Copenhagen's cultural elite.

Conclusion

During his own lifetime, Hans Christian Andersen tried to control his image and the narrative of his life story, writing multiple autobiographies and censoring information about himself that detracted from the image he wanted to project. Beginning with Georg Brandes, many scholars have attempted to put their own spin on Andersen's biography. However, as Stanley Fish reminds us, biographies are highly subjective, reflecting a particular scholar's view of the biographical subject. As was the case with Brandes's explanation of Andersen's childlike genius, such interpretations can be very influential in shaping subsequent constructions of the subject's biographical identity. The same principle applies to biopics, which are able to disseminate a particular image of the biographical subject to an immense global audience almost instantaneously.

The two recent American and Scandinavian biopics dealing with Hans Christian Andersen that we have examined reflect differing views of Andersen's nature and his relationship to his native country. Both films evoke Brandes's view of Andersen's literary genius stemming from his ability to appeal to the sensibilities of children, but they diverge in terms of the extent to which they allow the character of Andersen to mature beyond a juvenile state. The Hallmark Entertainment film treats Andersen more superficially; Andersen's character never moves beyond his naïveté, his juvenile behavior, or preoccupation with his own imagination. As a result, the film depicts Andersen as a socially ignorant—but exceptionally creative—author who is unable to escape his adolescence. *Unge Andersen* also uses Brandes's characterization of Andersen as a way to depict him during his early days under the tutelage of Rector Meisling, but the film contrasts this young, naive image of Andersen with an elderly, more somber version of Andersen's character. Andersen's childlike behavior is portrayed as merely a part of Andersen's journey to becoming a world-famous author.

Finally, the two films place unequal emphasis on Andersen's Danish background and cultural identity. As discussed above, one of the struggles involved with interpretations of Andersen's life and work concerns competing claims to control of his cultural and national identity. While American audiences may be less interested in the specific historic milieu in which Andersen was raised or the way in which Andersen's work reflects on his homeland, Danish filmmakers have a vested interest in emphasizing the Danish aspects of Andersen's story. It is not sufficient simply to note that the biopics we have examined conform to these expectations; we should also be aware of the ways in which both of them are trying to convey a particular image of Andersen, whether as a perennially childlike writer whose lively imagination allows him to speak directly to children, or as a venerable, mature author whose masterful works are informed by the challenges he faced in his youth and the creative coping strategies he developed along the way.

Works Cited

Andersen, H. C. (1908). *Mit Livs Eventyr*. Copenhagen: Gyldendal.

Brandes, G. (1984). [1869] "H. C. Andersen som Æventyrdigter." In *Danske klassikere*. København: Tiderne skifter.

Fish, S. (1999). "Just Published: Minutiae without Meaning." *New York Times*. September 7.

Hans Christian Andersen: My Life as a Fairytale. Dir. Philip Saville. 2003. Hallmark Entertainment.

Hjort, M. (2005). *Small Nation, Global Cinema*. Minneapolis: University of Minnesota Press.

Unge Andersen. Dir. Rumle Hammerich. 2005. Nordisk Film.

Index